The Power of Story

A Process of Renewal
for Therapists Who Treat Trauma

Bonnie J Collins

The Power of Story

A Process of Renewal
for Therapists Who Treat Trauma

Bonnie J. Collins, EdM, LCSW-R
and
Trina M. Laughlin, LCSW-R

Whole Person Associates
Duluth, Minnesota

Whole Person Associates
210 West Michigan Street
Duluth, MN 55802-1908
800-247-6789

The Power of Story
A Process of Renewal for Therapists Who Treat Trauma

Printed in the United States of America

10 9 8 7 6 5 4 3 2 1

ISBN 1-57025-215-7

Library of Congress Control Number: 2004110390

Dedication

To my mother, a writer in her own "write,"
who lulled me to sleep with the sound of her typing
throughout my childhood naps…

Thank you, Mom, with love,

Bonnie

To Margaret Beasley Parlato,
Janet Gleason Burke
and Victoria Bruno Leone,

the trinity of women who raised me…

Pieces of you are now pieces of me.

With love and gratitude,

Trina

Table of Contents

Special Acknowledgements

Linda Dinger, CSW-R,

a great source of creativity

Susan Rubendall, our editor,

for embracing our vision

Our families,

for their patience, support
and encouragement in this process

Prologue

Dear Fellow Therapists:

Providing therapeutic help to a person who has suffered a trauma puts the attending therapist at risk for vicarious trauma. Unlike burnout or compassion fatigue, vicarious trauma leaves the therapist with symptoms of either acute or posttraumatic stress responses. Therapists may become listless or hypervigilant and agitated. They may lose the desire to pursue their work or other activities in their lives that normally give them joy. Conversely, they may work night and day, desperately trying to find the "correct" approach to a particular case or personal life challenge. Relationships with family, friends and colleagues may suffer. For some, a pervasive sense of inadequacy begins to paralyze them and makes them inflexible in their work. Vicarious trauma presents in more ways than we need to elaborate on for the purposes of this book. Like the trauma responses in our clients, vicarious trauma is very real and very troubling. Vicarious trauma negatively impacts trauma therapists in mind, body and spirit.

 In this book, we provide a self-care process that can help prevent and alleviate vicarious trauma. The stories we tell illustrate and acknowledge that the very nature of trauma therapy exposes therapists to vicarious trauma. The stories also provide hope and encouragement to those who are story listeners.

One of the primary benefits we offer clients is our presence as a listening and validating human receptacle for their stories of trauma. Often our clients have kept their stories hidden deep within the confines of their minds, bodies and souls. Clients may feel that their stories are too terrible to repeat, not only to themselves but also to a listener. They may have decided that if they don't speak of them, these events can no longer hurt them or anyone else. Some of our clients express their stories in chronic illnesses like gastrointestinal irritability or pulmonary weak points. For these clients their bodies tell their stories.

As trauma therapists, it is an honor to help our clients feel safe enough to tell us their stories as an avenue to being set free. We, the therapists, help them break through their fear and shame so they can express their stories to us. We often unconsciously, or even deliberately, embrace their pain as we validate them as people who have been victims of trauma. We help them see that they are not responsible for what happened to them, and as we do this, we connect with them at the places they've felt most vulnerable. In the sharing of their story with us, their burden is diminished. The burden carried by one is now shared by two.

Unfortunately, we, as therapists, often take these stories of pain and suffering and lock them away within ourselves. We do this because, as professionals, we must treat our clients with respect and confidentiality. We are supposed to be the agents of hearing, not the agents of telling. While trauma therapists must be professional, they must also find ways to release from themselves the fragments of trauma that stick to them in the form of fear, grief, doubt and anger.

At a party, we observe a guest describing a car accident. He tells how traumatizing it was for him, and surrounding listeners respond with concern, compassion and support. We, the trauma therapists, stand in the background wishing we could share the many stories we know of trauma and victimization. Surely the stories we could tell would be met with the same concern, compassion and support. We often wish we could share the traumas we hear from our clients with people who would offer us that compassion and concern they offered the victim of the car accident.

For many reasons, we cannot do this. Short of very good clinical supervision and consultation with colleagues in the privacy of a work environment, we have no way to release shards of trauma that pierce our minds, bodies and spirits much like they had the minds, bodies and spirits of our clients. We, the authors, have become aware that when we do find support and relief from the trauma we absorb from our clients, it involves sharing this trauma in the form of a story with a colleagues who usually have stories of their own. Within these stories, there is always a bit about the client and a bit about the therapist. We have come to realize in the telling of these stories how much other people's traumas have affected us. To deny this is to invite vicarious trauma. To be aware of this and to give it a name helps us cope with it.

Keep in mind that the aforementioned relief is felt only when the relationship between the listener and the teller is good. Quite frankly, it often is difficult to find within our profession a relation-ship that allows for this kind of sharing. The supervision most common in our field often doesn't encourage this level of trust. Even with our belief in a strength-based model of doing therapy, the supervision for such therapy is administrative and solution–fo-cused. There is an imbalance between the focus on our clients and ourselves. But we, the authors, know that it is impossible to take the therapist out of the mix. If we were not important players in the exchange, our clients wouldn't be going to a trauma therapist in the first place.

That is why we decided to write this book. In the course of meet-ing on a regular basis and case conferencing together, we began to share more deeply how a particular case affected us personally. The meaning of our meetings began to change. In the exchange of stories, each of us discovered renewed energy for the work that we do. In listening to each other's stories, we shared each other's sorrows and celebrated each other's victories. We were amazed that we would often arrive at our meeting place exhausted and perhaps agitated but would leave energized, excited and hopeful. We discovered in the validation and empathy we gave to each other, places of similarity.

Whether we meet in a restaurant or walk in the mall or reach for the phone, a healing quality exists in all of our conversations. We affirm for one another that to work with a human being who has been traumatized, we must immerse ourselves in that person's experience. We emphatically acknowledge that there is a danger in that belief. Trauma begets trauma. By their very nature, the circumstances that make something qualify as traumatic push humans beyond their normal coping mechanisms.

Therapists are human too. When we hear the unhearable, when we paint a mental picture of the unseeable, we push ourselves beyond our normal range of coping as well. But when we share the pain we have heard with one another—much as we embraced the gift in the trauma for our clients—we become heartened to do it again. We have come to believe that other trauma therapists also need to dissipate their pain, share their successes, collectively weep for their losses and free themselves from the extra baggage that we all so willingly carry for our clients.

Now when we present seminars on how to cope with vicarious trauma, we read one of our stories to our audience, which almost immediately triggers stories from them. Everyone involved in this process has found the idea of recording stories in a journal of healing to be exciting. Thus, the birth of this book.

We would like you, the reader, to experience these stories. We hope that you, like participants in our seminars, will find that these stories trigger your own. This story-sharing process is not a new idea. People have been sharing stories since the beginning of communication. As therapists, we are fortunate to be story listeners on a daily basis. We now see the healing benefit in being storytellers as well.

The individuals in this book are real, and the stories are true. Through many rewrites, we have disguised all identities. All names, life circumstances and details have been changed. In essence, the individuals in these stories are a composite of many different people. Some of the people are you; some of the people are us; for spiritual moments are universal.

"There have been great societies that
did not use the wheel,
but there have been no societies
that did not tell stories."

Ursula LeGuin

Part One

On Being Real

Set Aside the Rules

Like a board game,
The rules are handed down to story listeners
"We must not cry!"
"We must not react!"
"We must not bleed!"

Life, however, is not a board game
Sometimes we do go to jail without passing go
Cheaters often win
There are no monopolies on tragedy
Life resists the rules.

Stories are the doorways to the teller's soul
Within the listening,
We often cry
We sometimes embrace
It is our honor to be real.

Being Real and the
Risk for Vicarious Trauma

We acknowledge with appreciation the training we have received from our mentors and teachers. Their teachings are the basis of our work and provide a solid structure and foundation from which we operate. We also thank the many clients we've encountered who have allowed us to take that foundation and make it come alive. The stories in this section are about growing up, about connecting with people and about becoming really real in our chosen work.

There are many types of therapy. Some of them are so theoretically structured that all the "coloring ends up inside the lines." We believe that it is possible to provide a substantive therapeutic experience by reflectively listening, asking about our client's feelings and by mirroring the client's pace and tone. These are rule-following treatment techniques. In all honesty, following these rules can provide some protection from vicarious trauma.

If you believe, as we do, that therapy works best when it is based on the relationship between therapist and client, you are at greater risk for vicarious trauma. The lessening of pain for the client occurs most frequently when the therapist is touched in a personal way by the client's story. We've found that when we expose our real selves during therapy, the outcome for both the client and the therapist changes. In our opinion, it changes for the better.

We are, therefore, confronted with a choice of recipes for therapy. We can make our therapeutic cake with butter, whole eggs, sugar and melted chunks of pure chocolate, or we can substitute oil, egg whites, artificial sweeteners, and a bean substitute that sort of tastes like chocolate. Each recipe has costs and benefits. One may be better for your health but lacks rich texture and taste. The other tastes magnificent but eaten too often has tremendous health risks. We will not mislead you. Becoming the "real ingredient" therapist places you at higher risk for vicarious trauma. What we propose in this book, however, is that real ingredient therapy does not have to be harmful as long as you prescribe for yourself a process parallel to what you recommend for your clients. Tell your story! Let the trauma out. Let the story bear the burden of the trauma, not the therapist.

In this section of the book, you will see that we put ourselves at risk by allowing ourselves to be personally touched by our clients' trauma.

We are pleased to present you with:

A Mother's Thanks

Godmothers

The Dance of Birth

I'm Not Black

Who Mirrors Who?

Mapmaker

A Mother's Thanks

Bonnie

Therapy with this couple began in an ordinary way. I made certain assumptions right away. It was the wife (as usual) who called for couples therapy, and (as usual) she wanted to bring her husband in since "he is the one with the problem." I'd been doing couples therapy for a long time, and I took pride in my ability to predict the needs of people even during their first phone call. This case, however, was designed to keep me humble. The woman seemed no different from many who had called. She wanted better communication between herself and her husband. She said he was withdrawing from her; they never talked anymore; or when they did, it was an argument. Their sex life was nonexistent, and there was no joy in their life together.

As usual, I invited them to an initial session and asked them to bring a definition of the problem as both of them saw it along with a list of the strengths in their relationship that might help them deal with the problem.

They arrived at the appointed time, and I found them in the waiting room where they had been silently staring into their coffee cups with an intensity that allowed them to avoid seeing each other or any one else in the room.

Ann was in her early 30s with short curly hair and sunglasses perched on the top of her head. She had big eyes and tanned skin, which, in combination with her high cheekbones and white teeth, gave her a healthy, pretty look. She sat with her long legs crossed under a flower print skirt and looked up with an open smile as I entered the room.

Jack looked older than his wife, perhaps in his 40s. He, too, was good-looking and athletic. He was neatly dressed in khakis and sneakers topped by a black tee shirt. He did not look up as openly as his wife did but instead scanned me quickly as if he were looking for trouble.

My first impressions of new couples are an important part of the therapeutic process for me, and I always make note of them. Intuitively, I felt their lack of connection to each other as well as her eagerness to give this process a try and his resistance, which I've learned over the years, is really self-protection.

This impression was confirmed further as she stood, introduced herself and reached to shake my hand. He remained seated and simply nodded his head in my general direction as she introduced him to me. I smiled at each of them and extended my hand to him. He shook it reluctantly and rather weakly. I offered them more coffee, which she declined and which he took readily, almost as though he wanted to delay the beginning of a process for which he wasn't quite ready.

I then ushered them into the therapy room and suggested that they sit wherever looked most comfortable to them. They chose to sit in chairs opposite each other rather than on the couch, where they might be physically closer.

At this point I always offer my clients a moment of silence to let them get settled and adapt to a new environment. I busy myself with paperwork but watch what each of them might do with this moment. In this case, Ann used it to settle in a chair and then to fuss with her skirt, her hair and her position in the chair. Jack, on the other hand, continued the behavior he began in the waiting room, which was to study me further and scan the environment. I watched him survey the room, appearing to take in all the details as if he were checking for defects or looking for danger.

As I took my seat, I went to work trying to make them feel as comfortable as possible in a setting that often provokes anxiety. Ann warmed to my attempts immediately by sharing with me how much she loved her husband though he was not himself these days. She explained that he was tense, short-tempered and withdrawn when he was not jumping down her throat. As she spoke of these worries, Jack braced himself as though he was being attacked.

When I turned to him to draw him into the conversation and get an idea of how he saw the marriage problem, my paperwork fell out of my lap. As Jack described the problem, stating that his wife was making mountains out of molehills, I reached down to pick it up and glancing at it briefly, saw that I had written during the intake that he was a Vietnam veteran. I began to study this man more intensely and saw a much younger face than the one actually looking at me. In its place, I saw a young soldier in an awful war. And then I thought of my two sons, twelve and fourteen years old at the time, who had no idea what war might be like. It occurred to me that it was because of this man and men like him that maybe, just maybe, my sons would not have to go to a strange place and fight with little understanding of what they were fighting for. This thought was so powerful my eyes filled with tears. I felt such deep gratitude for what this man had done that I stopped him in his defense of his role in his marriage and said, "I know what I am about to say has nothing to do with why you are here today; or maybe it has everything to do with why you are here today; but I just want to thank you for going to war in defense of us, your fellow citizens. I hope that because of you and those like you that my sons will not have to be soldiers. Thank you for trying to make this world a better place in which to live."

He stared at me and burst into tears, sobbing as I have never heard anyone sob except in moments of deep grief. I waited with tears in my own eyes; looking at Ann, I realized she was quietly crying too. We all sat in our individual sadness for a long time. Finally, Jack spoke up. With softened features, he gazed directly into my eyes with a look that touched my soul and said, "No one has ever expressed a 'thank you' for what I went through over there. All I came home with was nightmares, flashbacks, guilt and an addiction to any substance that would numb the pain and help me avoid what I did to survive a war I didn't understand. To even begin to contemplate that I might have done something worthwhile over there seems impossible, but to think I may have prevented the next generation of boys from having to experience war helps give meaning to what I had to do. I thank you from the bottom of my heart."

He reached over and grabbed my hand with a touch that communicated his gratitude even more than his words.

How to go on? He took care of that too. He reached for his wife, and they stood and hugged each other with such intimacy that I left the room. I waited in my own waiting room for them to leave the privacy of their connection to each other. They greeted me with smiles and thanked me for such a healing session. They scheduled their next session for the following week and left holding hands.

I went home and hugged my boys with tears in my eyes. At twelve and fourteen, they were naturally a bit resistant to this emotional demonstration of affection.

The following week I got a phone call from Jack canceling their next session. He said, "I really wanted to come back because you helped me feel so much better about myself, but it is because I feel so empowered that I have no more nightmares. My wife and I have renewed our sex life and are talking so much our kids can't get a word in edgewise. I will always remember your honoring of me, and I will try to live the rest of my life as though I earned that honor."

So much for "therapy as usual!"

Godmothers

Trina

Jeanne and her mother, Pearly, had a complex relationship. They loved each other tremendously. Jeanne told me things about her mother that she was exceptionally proud of. When she talked about Pearly putting herself through nursing school while raising a family, her eyes glazed over with a childlike awe, and her tone was strong and proud. Jeanne knew how she struggled with her own five children. She felt that meeting their needs forced her to put her own career pursuits on hold.

Pearly also loved Jeanne; she smiled when you said her daughter's name. When they were together, Pearly often had a hand on Jeanne's shoulder, and Pearly supportively invited her daughter to "get mad at me" during sessions.

After two years of working with Jeanne, she was starting to get in touch with the conflicted relationship she had with her Mom. She carried a great deal of anger toward Pearly. While Jeanne was growing up, Pearly had worked two jobs to support her children. She also supported her stay-at-home third husband.

Jeanne was third oldest and the first girl of seven children. When she was eight years old, while Pearly was at work, Jeanne's stepfather repeatedly raped her. He pinned her on the bed, forcing her to look at the loaded shotgun that rested against the bedroom dresser. He told her he would use that shotgun on her mother if she ever told.

The sexual attacks began on Jeanne's eighth birthday. The first time he assaulted her, he told her it was his birthday present to her. He said, "I have the best gift for you, I'm gonna make you into a woman."

It wasn't until eight years later that Jeanne told anyone, and that was only after she had heard numerous times from her mother how bad she was for being sullen all the time. She remembers Pearly saying, "Mama's special girl has turned into a hell child. What is wrong with you girl?"

Jeanne loved her mother. She remembered bedtime stories on the nights Pearly was at home; she loved her smell—she still had a blanket from childhood that she had sprayed with her mother's perfume.

Jeanne also hated her mother for not being there for her and for not knowing that special girls just don't turn bad unless something bad happened to them.

One day, twenty-six months after we began working, Jeanne sat in my office. We had reduced our visits to once a month. Jeanne no longer needed to shamefully hide out in her house, where she couldn't muster up the energy to pick anything up or do dishes or even cook. Today she was enrolled in two college courses. Her children had been returned to her and were no longer at risk of removal as they had been so many times in the past. It struck me that her six-foot-two frame seemed comfortable and relaxed in the chair. For a year and a half she had sat perched in that chair, sitting only on the front three inches. She had always postured in such a way that she could easily flee the session or pounce on me if I were to push too hard. In the first seven months we worked together, she "fired" me about fifteen times. I pretended I didn't understand the firing or sometimes just ignored her. During those periods when I had been fired, I often drove through the neighborhood and picked her up for a session rather than have her not show up.

The times she refused to get in the car, we talked on the front porch or in the hallway. She had a session anyway, and it gave her needed power to be able to tell me no. I allowed her to get angry with me, to say no to me and to "act up." Jeanne got to misbehave and still was not abandoned.

I thought about many of our past ups and downs as she was talking. It was as though I had daydreamed off, and when I returned, a powerful, independent, attractive, soft-spoken young woman sat before me. She was such a contrast to the frazzled, angered, disheveled woman-child I had seen so many times previously. She sat fully relaxed in the chair. Her makeup was meticulous. Her formerly splotchy brown complexion had a warm bronzy glow. Bright red lipstick not only made her lips stand out but also made her face a showcase for her large, brown, gentle eyes. I remember thinking, "My God, this woman is gorgeous; she looks like a model." It was particularly significant because one of Jeanne's self-blaming behaviors was to make herself as unattractive as she possibly could. She always feared that if she made herself attractive, people would continue to molest her. Her belief system said, "It was my fault because I was pretty."

On this day, Jeanne was more than pretty, she was beautiful! A couple weeks prior to this session, I had validated her new ability to maintain long-term relationships. Jeanne had been through numerous relationships, many of which were abusive. This was all beginning to change. She told me in a phone conversation that she and Hank were going to be married even though Hank had probably been "fired" more times than I had. She said, "You know, you and Hank were like a couple of bulldogs. Every time I tried to make you go away, you just ended up staying. It used to make me really mad; then it finally dawned on me that you believed in me. You believed in me before I did, when it seemed like nobody ever had before. You were like a godmother. You know in church how a godmother agrees to help the child stay on a good path and agrees to be an example of what is right?"

I acknowledged that I did know, that in my religion godmothers signed up for the same duties. I thanked Jeanne for the compliment, and I began saying all the "right" things. I told her that she was the one who did all the work. While my mouth was speaking all the correct therapeutic words, my heart was agreeing. I did feel like I had been like a godmother. Many times it would have been easier to give up on Jeanne and to stamp her file "NONCOMPLI-ANT- CLOSED," but I didn't. We had developed a special bond, one that should not have been invalidated by me talking from textbooks. But we were closing her case at this session, and it seemed easier for me to drop all the real things I was to her and she was to me and fly on automatic pilot.

Fortunately it dawned on me that that would have been a disservice to us both. I listened to Jeanne, and I thanked her from my heart. Jeanne went on and said, "Hank and I have been talking, and you know I'm pregnant. This summer when the baby is born, we would like for you to be her godmother."

Jeanne was more comfortable with me telling her that I couldn't do that than I was. According to our agency policy, I wouldn't be able to have such a relationship with a present or former client. I truly loved this young woman, and over the long time we worked together, I had become involved with many extended family members. Some of her other children were in children's support groups that I ran, and I knew and loved them as well. As much as I personally wanted to say yes, this would have represented a dual relationship that I could not have. Jeanne understood completely and said she sort of knew I would have to say no before she asked, but she had wanted me to know how much she thought of me. She said, "When I was small, I was left in the care of someone who could not be trusted, I want you to know that if I were to leave one of my children in someone's care who could be trusted, that person would be you." We embraced, and I assured her that I would be at the church service for the christening, even though I could not be the godmother.

The invitation came to the office. As I read the location of the Baptist church in the city, I was amused to think how once again history repeats itself. I had a vision of myself being the only white face in a sea of well-dressed African-American friends and relatives. One thing I have always been aware of is the special care black people put into their clothing for church and celebrations. I laughed as I thought of myself hatless, basic and white, sitting amongst ebony masterpieces wearing flower-bedecked hats and bright-colored dresses. I had my own ebony masterpieces growing up.

When I was a child my father owned a hotel, and for a time we lived in a suite of rooms there. Both Mom and Dad worked very hard at the hotel, and often when they were working, I would wander around. The ballrooms and the restaurants were my playgrounds. I could imagine myself dancing in the ballrooms, and there was something comforting about the smell of mahogany and leather in the English Grill Room. Yet many times I found myself lonely and lost, and I missed having friends to play with. One day when the housekeeping staff was finishing our suite, Marion, the head housekeeper, suggested that I tag around with her. She let me empty the wastebaskets and even let me bounce a few times on the beds in each room before she changed the bed linens. We would end up back in the housekeeping office where the loud chatter and energy between the women made me feel safe. Somehow I became a permanent addition to this group of new friends. They helped me with homework and talked to me about life. They helped me feel safe and comfortable when forced integration and bussing brought twenty or so black children to my school. They helped me learn how to be a friend to those twenty children and how to help them feel safe and comfortable in their new alien surroundings.

The hotel was torn down in 1968, and I lost touch with my friends. I thought of them often but never saw them or even talked to them. Four years later I graduated from a private high school, which unfortunately had no African-American students. But on graduation day, that made it much easier to pick out the three ebony goddesses with matching hats, handbags and suits. There they were in the tenth row: Marion, Harriet and Laverne, the mother goddesses who helped me grow up. After the ceremony I found them and excitedly hugged them. I blurted out, "But how did you know to come?" Marion leaned into me as we hugged and said, "A child's fairy godmothers know everything."

I wrote out Jeanne's card before I left for the christening. Among all the congratulations and best wishes I wrote, " I may not be able to be your baby's actual godmother, but I know a few things about fairy godmothering. Thank you for making me feel special and believing in me." Later that day, after the ceremony, Jeanne put the most magical little being into my arms and proudly said, "I'd like you to meet Trina Aisha."

The Dance of Birth

Bonnie

I'm not doing this again!" she said as she sat in front of me. Tears streamed down her face as she balanced a baby on her lap. The child, who was about 18 months old, looked back at her Mom's face and then turned to reach for me while clapping her hands. I took Amber from her mom and enjoyed her look of delight. I ran my fingers through her wonderfully curly hair as I tried to give my attention to both mother and daughter.

I struggled with enjoying the baby while showing compassion for her mother, whose crying increased after I removed the child from her lap. Carol began to tell me about how horrible her labor and delivery was when she had this child.

"It was just awful, and I'm so frightened of going through it again," she said between sobs. "I'm just two months pregnant now, and I'm so afraid that I think I want an abortion, but I feel so ashamed about wanting that. My husband is no help. He tells me that it's up to me, and whatever decision I make he will support me. I suppose that sounds great, but I'm so angry at him for leaving this all up to me."

As I sat playing with the baby and listening to her, she went on: "My first pregnancy was fine. In fact, I rather enjoyed it. My family gave me a lot of attention, and all of them were so excited about having a new baby in our midst. I haven't even told anyone that I'm pregnant this time because I can't be happy about it. I don't want to go through that birth process again. I have nightmares about it. I was so out of control and in so much pain. No one helped me at the hospital. In fact, the nurse either hollered at me for screaming so loud or just left me alone and didn't respond when I called for her. I can't describe to you how awful it was."

I commented, "I think you are describing it all too well, and I am truly sorry you had to go through that."

She continued, "My husband just sat there or paced in the hall. He was no help at all. I refuse to go through that again."

By now, Carol was pacing around my office wringing her hands and sobbing loudly. Amber, on my lap, seemed mesmerized by her mother. She watched her pace and sat very still. I couldn't help but worry that it was traumatizing to her to see her mother so upset. Moreover, I wondered how often she might hear this story as she was growing up and what that might do to her. I was torn between helping the mom sort this all out and comforting the baby, who at this point seemed to be in a trance.

Just as I was about to ask Carol to sit down and do some deep breathing for the sake of her child, she seemed to run out of steam. She did sit down, blew her nose and reached for her baby.

"So that's why I'm here," she said. "I want you to support me through an abortion and help me with the grief afterwards." I was impressed that she knew she would need help with her grief. Obviously, she had thought a lot about this.

I said, "I can do that, but would you be willing to look at alternatives to abortion with me?"

"I think I've done that on my own," she quickly responded. "I've been struggling with this since the moment I knew I was pregnant.

I can't see any alternatives."

Just then, the baby patty-caked and squealed with delight as she bounced on her mom's lap. Carol hugged her and patty-caked with her. As she held her child, she turned to me. Looking me directly in the eyes, she said, "Please help me. I'm at my wit's end, and I don't know what to do. I'm very uncomfortable with abortion, but the birth process I experienced with this one was just too traumatic for me to go through it again."

"I suggest that we meet again," I said, seeing that she was ambivalent enough to work well in therapy. When people are too rigid about what they want from therapy, it often doesn't work. Ambivalence leaves people open to options.

"I want to help you, but I'm not sure I'm willing to start our therapy with helping you go through an abortion. Sometimes that can be even more traumatic than labor and delivery. Would you consider coming back again and looking at what else we might come up with to avoid another traumatic delivery?"

She agreed to return but said, "I have doubts about alternatives."

As she stood to go, I was aware for the first time how tall she was and how gracefully she moved as she swung her daughter over her shoulder. The baby laughed when I tickled her and waved bye-bye as they left the room.

Carol came back to her next session without little Amber. I missed the charming child, but I was glad Carol came alone. Therapy doesn't go well unless it takes place in a private setting. Having no interruptions or distractions encourages both the client and the clinician to focus. I know from experience that mothers have a hard time doing that when they bring their children to a session. Besides, the distraction of that darling, curly-headed little girl was too much for me, a grandma-wanna-be.

Carol and I began to work. I once again noticed her physical appearance, her long legs and the way she moved even while sitting. She used her hands in an animated way when she talked and tipped her head gracefully to one side as she listened. She wrapped her legs around each other and pointed her toes as she sat across from me.

"Tell me about yourself," I said, "Who are you Carol? What in your life gives you energy and meaning?"

Carol seemed intrigued by these questions and sat looking down at her hands, quietly folded in her lap, as she seemed to think deeply about how to answer.

"Well," she said, "I get energy and meaning in my life from dancing. I've always danced. My dad is a dancer, too, and we own a dance studio together. It's in my house, and I teach ballet and tap and modern dance, mostly to kids. I love kids. That's why this abortion idea is very upsetting to me. I love to dance, and I love to perform and put on recitals with my students. It's such fun. I never tire of it."

"Wow," I said, "what a wonderful way to give your life meaning. Let's look at this a minute. You speak with so much energy about your love of dance. Could we somehow get you to love the birth process as much? Could you ever see that same energy put into the delivering of your baby?"

"Ha!" she said in a sarcastic tone. "Never could that happen. When I dance I am in charge. I know what I'm doing. I don't feel helpless, and I'm certainly not in pain. There is no comparison."

Not to be discouraged, I said, "But maybe we could choreograph the birth process just like you choreographed a dance. Are there any similarities?"

She uncrossed her long legs, stood up, walked past my chair and began pacing. I noticed that even her pacing was graceful. She moved like a dancer, taking steps with her toes pointed out and turning around with a swirl as she reached the end of the room.

Pacing seems to be her thing, I thought to myself. This woman needs to move as she thinks. It made sense. She is a dancer.

"Lets take a walk," I said. "You obviously do your best thinking when you are moving. There's a park near here where we can walk together."

She didn't even hesitate and practically lunged for the door. "I hope I can keep up with you," I said with a smile. She was 20 years my junior and at least 5′ 9″ compared to my 5′ 1″ frame.

She laughed and said, "You can keep up. I'll choreograph our walk so we establish a rhythm that works for both of us."

We spent the next six sessions of therapy walking. During that time together, Carol planned a birth process as though it were a dance recital. She was a great choreographer and took this on as a challenge. She got so into the orchestration of it that she said one day, "How could I have ever thought about an abortion?" Neither of us needed to answer that question.

I saw myself like a stage manager or director behind the scenes as her "Dance of Birth" began to take shape.She would come to therapy every week with new ideas about how this birth would take place. She worked with both the idea of making it different from her first birth experience and making it a celebratory event.

She found a midwife with whom she could talk ahead of time about her need not to experience trauma again. The midwife agreed to help her make this birth different in as many ways as possible.

She also found a hospital where she could have a "normal bed" as she called it and a private room. She wanted to deliver in a place where she could bring flowers and decorations, a room where she could play music during labor and have a rocking chair in which to rock the baby once it was born.

Carol and I established, as she had promised, a good rhythm on our weekly therapeutic walks. As she entered her ninth month of pregnancy, we were still walking. On one of those walks, she asked if I would consider being present at the birth of this child. I felt choreographed into the celebration, and it was with great delight that I agreed to take part in this event. As a therapist, was this breaking the boundaries my profession encouraged me to keep? Maybe it was, but how could I say no? This was about life much more than it was about therapy!

As the time got closer, Carol became more eager. This was quite a contrast to her first birth experience. As a therapist I was glad for her, but I was concerned for that first child, Amber, who at two had to be absorbing some of her mother's excitement about this whole thing just as she must have absorbed how traumatized her mother had felt at her own birth. Could she be part of the "Dance of Birth" too?

"Could we figure out a way to include Amber is this celebration?" I asked Carol on one of our walks.

She obviously hadn't thought of that, but she grabbed the idea and danced with it as only she could. She decided, after checking with the midwife and her husband, that as soon as the baby was born, Amber would be brought into the room and, under the of supervision of Daddy, she would give the new child its first bath.

The moment of birth arrived! Of course, it was the middle of the night. Dad called me at 2AM and asked me to come soon. I was immediately wide awake and quickly on my way to the hospital. I smiled to myself as I drove, asking myself if this was what I thought

I would be doing years ago when I decided to become a therapist? Absolutely not! It's better than what I thought being a therapist would be like!

I got to the hospital just in time. The attendant gave me a pair of scrubs (which I saved to this day), and I entered the room where candles were lit, the lights were low, and music was playing softly in the background.

Carol was in labor and smiling. She welcomed me with a hug between contractions, and Dad hovered around the bed like a bee around a flower. The baby crowned; the doctor and midwife were there; and out came Angela with a healthy cry—right to the beat of the music and with a big cheer from everyone.

The doctor held her up for all to see. I knew my solo in this dance came when I was asked to cut the umbilical cord. What a moment! With tears streaming down my cheeks and a big smile on my face, I did the honors.

Amber was brought in to wash Angela with Dad's help, and Mom cracked open a bottle of champagne as she moved to the rocking chair to wait for the baby to be brought to her.

It was five o'clock in the morning and I had just cut an umbilical chord and sipped champagne in celebration of a new life. The midwife lit a candle on a birthday cake that Carol had also choreographed into this dance. As we all sang happy birthday to this new little angel, I knew this was the best therapy I had ever been part of.

PS. Carol went on to have two more babies in two more wonderful "Birth Dances." She still owns a dancing school, where she shares her enthusiasm for life with many children.

I'm Not Black

Trina

It was a warm September day. There were plenty of people out, even more people as I crossed some invisible line of demarcation that changed our community from the white residential neighborhoods to the predominantly black and Hispanic "hood." I had accepted an internship at a community agency that served predominantly people of color, and I was really working hard to get with the new politically correct lingo. When I told my friends and family where I was going to be working for the next year, my automatic pilot wanted to say, "All of my clients and coworkers are black," but my School of Social Work training assured me that I should say, "all of my clients and coworkers are people of color."

The warm sun felt good on my face as I walked from the parking lot to the building. I remember thinking how well it matched the warmth I felt inside about the work I was doing and the people I was doing it with. Three weeks ago, when I started here, it was a completely foreign experience for me to be in a setting of about fifty black people and only one white person—me. I felt conspicuous, which made me feel uncomfortable. I thought people were going to watch my every move and judge those moves as bad—not different—definitely bad.

The first day I walked into the agency, I thought about Bwana Daniels and Zora Dee. Bwana and Zora were two of the twenty or so black kids that were bussed into my elementary school back in 1966. I was amazed that it never dawned on me back then how lonely and different they must have felt. I tried to convert my new feelings into learning. In a very small measure, I was learning what it felt like to be racially conspicuous. I felt guilty for even making the comparison, however, because the measure was so very small.

I was grateful today that those feelings of discomfort were gone. I had no idea where they went, and they weren't nearly as conscious in their going as they had been in their coming. I just began to fit. I fit in the agency; I fit in the neighborhood, I began to fit better in my own skin.

I handed Henry a dollar and purposely let my hand rest in his a moment longer than needed as I gave him the bill. We started doing that a couple of days ago; he seemed to like the momentary physical connection, and I did too. That warm rush came over me again as I remembered the day I met Henry.

For a student, one of the pluses of working at the Urban Agency was that parking was free. There was a big lot across the street just for our staff. That first day, as I got out of my car, my insides began to tremble as a dirty, homeless man approached me. It was late August, yet this bearded, disheveled individual was wearing a sweatshirt and a winter coat. His pants looked as though they had been urinated in. He had one unlaced sneaker and one tie-up shoe. He carried a cardboard sign, "Will work for food."

In a friendly enough tone, he said, "You're new here." I acknowledged that I was as I began to walk, more swiftly than usual, toward the building. He continued, "You might want to contract with me to keep an eye on your car, pretty bad neighborhood you know." I remember saying something curt, like, "I'm all set thanks, not today." I know I said it with my back to him, and my words probably dropped like verbal ice cubes as I continued to speed-walk toward the building. Whenever I could, throughout the course of the day, I looked out the agency window to be sure the homeless man wasn't vandalizing my car. As I left the building that night, a few other staff members were going out at the same time. They weren't with me, just near me. I heard Henry speak to one of them and say, "Evening James, just wanted you to know that I won't be here tomorrow. I have to go recertify so be careful with your car." James responded, "Thanks for letting me know Henry." That was the first time it dawned on me that the Homeless Man had a name, and his name was Henry.

The next couple of mornings, I watched my coworkers. Most of them stopped and spoke for a moment with Henry; some gave him some change. Olivia, my office-mate, gave him a muffin one morning. The first day I spoke with Henry I was probably motivated to do so because I wanted to fit in, I figured that if my coworkers were speaking to him, I'd better start doing it too. Perhaps it would help alleviate the feelings of being conspicuous that I had as I entered the building. By this time Henry had learned not to approach me. He had begun to keep a reasonable distance between himself and me, so in order to get with this fitting in thing, I actually had to walk up to him. He looked puzzled as I backtracked from the building toward him and said, "Good morning, you mentioned something about contracting with you to watch my car. How does that work?" He immediately smiled, and once again I found my initial judgments challenged. Henry had all his teeth, and they looked pretty darn good. I stood there chastising myself with "what did you expect? Is there some reason he shouldn't have his own teeth?" I really was struggling with doing it right, being a nonjudgmental social worker, fitting in and not being judged myself. Somewhere within that magical moment I had stumbled into, I was able to get out of my own way; I was able to say, "You know that first day when you walked up to me, I was scared. I guess I'm pretty leery of strangers, especially when the place is strange to me too."

My automatic pilot was scolding me, "What in God's name are you telling him that for? Just give him the dollar and fit in. Your goal is to fit in! My brain committee had to shut up momentarily in order to even hear what he was saying. "I'm sorry I frightened you. Sometimes I forget how scary I can look. I'm Henry. What's your name?" We spent a few minutes chatting as Henry spoke to Trina, and Trina spoke to Henry. I felt better, but I don't think at that moment that I knew why.

At any rate, the days passed and now, on this warm September morning, I felt good. I felt comfortable. Henry thanked me for the dollar and added that he really appreciated last night's newspaper.

Later that morning, I sipped coffee in my office as I put the finishing touches on a presentation I was doing for the parenting group I ran. I had made wonderful color-coded charts about developmental stages of children and the motor skills and communication styles they would have at certain ages. I looked at the charts with absolute pride. My clients that I had come to know over the last four weeks were going to love this.

Some of the parents were mandated to attend by Child Protective Services. Some came because it was a place to spend time and have a cup of coffee. Many really wanted to know how they could be better parents. They wanted to learn things about children that they never had an opportunity to know. I was slowly learning the whys of their coming as I read case files on the group members. That morning I read Marie's file. Marie had been referred to the parenting group from one of our other programs, Friends and Family of Murdered Children. Marie's seventeen-year-old son, Derrick, had been killed in a drive-by shooting as he walked home from a party held only five doors away from his house. Marie had three other children, and she was coming to the parenting class to find out how to keep them alive.

Marie came dutifully every week. She shared when it was appropriate. She paid attention to the presentation of the week. Sometimes it was about fire safety; sometimes it was about discipline; this week it was about developmental stages.

As I put the easel up and placed my first chart on it, I felt a queasy feeling in my stomach that I sometimes get when I am about to do something different than my norm, I had the same queasiness the day I told Henry that he originally had frightened me. I knew, however, that the queasy feeling was usually followed by truth and warmth, a very good warmth.

I turned toward the group and said, "You know what? I've been coming here for the last four or five weeks, and I've taken a lot for granted. You may or may not have noticed—but I guess you have noticed—that I'm not black. I'm not black; I'm not financially strapped; I've never had to navigate the child protective system or the welfare system. I have no idea what it feels like to let my child go to a party down the street and not have him come home because he got shot on the way. I don't think developmental charts mean a whole heck of a lot when there sometimes isn't enough money to put nutritious food on the table. How would it be if we just talk today? If you help me know what parenting is about for you, then I can tell you what it is about for me."

Marie was gently crying in the back row. Some of the other members were already moving the chairs from their straight rows into a circle. One member gestured to a seat next to her and said, "Please sit down and join us; let's talk." Parenting group went overtime that warm September day.

Who Mirrors Who?

Bonnie

I was tired. It had been a long day. I'd already seen five clients and had no lunch break. I was not up for another client but there was one more up for me. I took a few deep breaths as I sat still and counted to 60, giving myself an opportunity to renew my energy.

As I walked down the hall to the waiting room, I could see Dorothy sitting in the corner directly in my line of vision. She slouched, her chin to her chest, her hands draped over the arms of the chair in a limp posture. At first, I thought she might be asleep, but she looked up at me as I entered the room. She only looked up; her body remained still. She was wearing a dark sweater that stretched tautly over her big belly. Her pants were too short for her, and her feet were shoved into boots with worn heels.

Dorothy's appearance sent a message about how depressed she was. Having met with her several times already, I knew she was not grasping the hope for healing that I was trying to encourage in her. Our sessions were filled by her descriptions of how lousy she felt, how she didn't care about living any longer, how the medicine wasn't working and how she just wasn't getting better.

I wasn't feeling so great myself. I felt like I was running out of compassion for this woman, and of course, that is a sin to me. I'm a therapist. I'm supposed to have an endless amount of compassion for others. Shame on me!

Trying to muster up energy to connect with Dorothy, I forced a smile and signalled for her to follow me down the hall as I said with more energy than I felt, "Hello Dorothy. How are you on this beautiful sunny day?"

Dorothy didn't answer but slowly stood up with a big sigh. No greeting, no return smile, simply a big sigh. She lumbered along behind me as I led the way to my office.

I entered the room ahead of her and sat at my desk motioning for her to take her usual seat in the chair next to the desk. Dorothy always preferred this arrangement—me at the desk and her in the chair beside the desk.

The alternative is the cushioned chair or love seat, which I have arranged in a conversational circle. Most clients sit in that circle with me, and I feel it creates warmth and an opportunity to connect with each other in a way that sitting at a desk together does not. Dorothy never chose that arrangement. She declined whenever I suggested she might be more comfortable there. I certainly am more comfortable there, but I've accommodated her wish. I assumed she needed to be more formal to feel safe.

I turned to face her as she lowered her weight into the chair and asked again, "How are you?" I knew I was saying this in a monotone voice with little expression in my tone or on my face.

She responded simply, "I'm the same—no better."

I was already tired, and Dorothy was making me more tired. I felt frustrated, hopeless, and helpless, and I didn't know what to say. My own shoulders sloped. I put my elbow on the desk and held my head up with my hand, looking at her silently, hoping she would tell me more.

Dorothy's head came up; her body turned directly toward me; and she made direct eye contact.She slammed her fist on the desk and said in a loud, angry voice, "What is your problem? You are supposed to give me hope, empower me and make me feel better. And there you sit, like a lump, hardly able to hold up your own head. What's the matter with you? You're no help to me. You look awful. Do you have to lean on your desk as though you are about to go to sleep? You're not talking to me at all. This certainly isn't helpful." With that, she stood up more quickly than I had ever seen her move and headed for the door.

I was in shock. Besides being startled at her actions, I was amazed at Dorothy's sudden energy. She looked so different. Her eyes were dancing like sparks from a firecracker. She was crunching up her face and turning red. She stopped at the door, and I could hear her breathing hard as she turned back to look at me as though she was giving me one last chance.

I felt caught, ashamed and miserable. I was guilty. She was right. I was not being attentive to her. I was all out of compassion. How could I get back on track with this woman?

A moment of insight landed on me like a message from above. I realized that because I was vulnerable due to my own tiredness, I was absorbing Dorothy's feelings, her posture and her passivity. I, too, was feeling hopeless. It was as if I had caught her depression.

Dorothy continued to stare at me. She seemed to be holding me accountable for my lack of support for her and was waiting for my defense.

It only took me a moment to decide to tell her the truth.

"I'm depressed," I said, clearly and directly in a loud voice. "I feel like I caught it from you! It's not your fault really, but I am tired today and so I think I am vulnerable to feeling like you feel—hopeless, helpless, with no energy. Seeing you in your depression made me feel like I'm depressed, too.

Had I said too much? Was I getting too personal? I shut up, shut down and held my breath. I was probably going to be fired as her therapist.

Dorothy continued to stare at me, but her eyes softened, and the muscles in her face slackened. She came back to her chair and sat down as she let out a long, slow breath.

"Is that how I look and act? Do I slouch like you just did? Do I look half-asleep to you? Am I silent, and do I send a message of hopelessness like you just projected?"

She paused as though she was taking it all in and then continued, "How awful I must appear to my family and friends and to you—all the people trying to help me." She grunted, covered her face with her hands and began to cry softly.

Through her sobs, she said, "I don't know how I'm going to get out of this, but thank you for the mirror you have provided for me to look at how I look to others. I have to change."

With desperation in her voice (which also sounded like motivation), Dorothy reached for my hand and said, "Please help me not look like you just looked."

Tears came to my own eyes, and I simply nodded and reached for my scheduling book, eager to set up another appointment in which we could really begin our work.

Dorothy asked to hug me as she stood up to go, and as we hugged, I felt the tiredness drain and found myself looking forward to our next time together.

After Dorothy left, I sat for a while at my desk, alone with my thoughts. Was I depressed? Was I on the edge of burnout? Did I have compassion fatigue, or was I being vicariously traumatized by Dorothy's trauma? Did I provide a mirror for Dorothy, or did she provide one for me? Dorothy was ready to move on and begin to really take care of herself. I needed to do the same. I reached for the phone and dialed my supervisor.

The Mapmaker

Trina

I was not prepared for Shaniqua. I had been to her apartment once before I was able to successfully open her case, but she wasn't there. The building was a high-rise for people with low incomes and was situated in a bad neighborhood. Off-duty police officers provided security at the lobby entrance door, and they scrutinized everyone who was coming and going. I felt uncomfortable having to provide the guard with my agency identification, which by association would identify Shaniqua as a person with specific issues. Quite frankly those issues were just none of his business. Maybe because of this information exchange, or merely because he was intrusive, he felt obligated to tell me that Shaniqua wasn't there because she had been arrested. He said, "We won't put up with much more of this, she's going to get her ass evicted. She attacked another tenant last night, and RPD hauled her ass out of here."

He seemed to want some sort of validation and waited expectantly for me to give him additional information about Shaniqua. He seemed genuinely annoyed when I simply said, "I'll try again later," and offered him nothing in the way of juicy gossip.

He had, however, been successful in getting me to mentally add the information he gave me to other background information. I mentally mulled over the intake material as I drove back to the office. The intake had read:

Shaniqua Young, 23-year-old African American female, recently had her two youngest children removed.

Children: Charles Owens, age 3, and Derrick Beasley, age 2, have been placed in temporary foster care as a result of mother's failure to protect. Shaniqua Young has been involved in numerous relationships in which there is domestic violence. The most recent involved the father of Derrick, who attacked Ms. Young while she was holding said infant, Derrick Owens. Ms. Young has two older children aged 8 and 7, who presently reside in Alabama.

Ms. Young's rights with her older children have been terminated due to similar neglect and an inability to find kinship care while Ms. Young served a prison sentence for felony assault. Ms. Young was convicted of felony assault in 1st for inflicting bodily harm on a seventeen-year-old tenant in her building. The seventeen-year-old sustained serious injury to her left hand as a result of Ms. Young biting her thumb to the point it was almost severed. Victim also received nine facial stitches as a result of being struck with a bottle.

I began to think how easy it would have been to buy into what the security officer said. I wasn't altogether certain that I wasn't afraid of this woman. I received the referral from our preventive unit because in a session Shaniqua told the preventive worker that as a child she had been sexually abused. No other details beyond that. Whatever else was going on—domestic violence, poverty, arrest, foster care, DSS issues—they hear "adult survivor of sexual abuse," and I get involved. I felt pleased and honored that my colleagues had begun to buy into my belief that childhood sexual trauma can shape and foster many issues in people's lives.

The following week I met with Shaniqua. She opened the door. As usual I had prepared myself to look up to make eye contact.

Most of the people I meet are taller than my 5′ 2″ frame. In this instance, as I shifted my glance downward, I could hear my mother's Irish whisper resonate in my head, "She's just a sprite of a thing." Shaniqua stood at least two inches shorter than me. She had on an absolutely spotless white sweatshirt that complimented her dark skin. I thought as she preceeded me into her apartment that if the clothes she wore were a size 0, they may still have been too big for her. Her closely cropped hair cut was an orangey color. Her smile was her most amazing feature. Cheshire cats would be put to shame by it. Not only was it ear to ear, but sometimes, as she turned her head, flashes of the gold crowns on her back teeth would glisten. Sometimes the flash looked light and magical, like the mischievous elfin sprite my mother was whispering about. At other times, it seemed sharp and dangerous, making me think of the seventeen-year-old's nearly severed thumb.

The first weeks of our relationship were marked by a dance of polar opposites. Sometimes Shaniqua was quiet, vulnerable and soft. She seemed to hang on my every word and on the words of other women in the group. She listened as we talked about worth and loss and about shame that did not belong to them. She was mesmerized by the new concept that she didn't have to be ashamed about being raped as a child. She allowed herself to get closer to me and to the other group members and told us how this was very different for her because she had always walked around afraid of people. She talked about needing to push people away and never get close.

We were able to laugh with her when we responded, "Gee, for a person who is so afraid, you sure don't look scared—most of the time you look pretty mad!" This observation culminated when, in about the fifth week of group, the soft, vulnerable Shaniqua no longer walked in the door. Instead, soft and vulnerable had been replaced with angry as hell. Her small frame rippled with amazing muscles that looked as if they were carved out of steel. Her jaw was tight, and her eyes had become dark and piercing.

She refused to do the feelings check-in that was a normal opening for our group.

I watched the other group members, all of whom had been victimized as children, become internally terrorized. They knew seething rage when they saw it. The connected, bonded atmosphere of the group was replaced with disjointed, isolating fear. The group was fragmenting before my eyes, with everyone escaping into their own protective cocoons. As I gently pressed Shaniqua, she threatened, "Don't mess with me if I don't want to talk. You fucking better hear it!"

She said these words in a hoarse whisper with her front teeth almost touching one another. As the words hissed through her clenched teeth, there was something more threatening about her quiet, simmering rage than if she had been hollering or throwing things. Also in a quiet tone, I responded, "I hear you, I was wondering if you would just tell me one thing?"

After a short pause, I continued, "If you know this is a talking group, and you clearly don't want to talk, why did you come today?" There was no response, just a greater tensing of her already wired frame.

I cautiously continued, "I was wondering if maybe you felt comfortable enough here that you finally wanted someone 'safe' to see your anger?"

Shaniqua looked at the floor and began to rock back and forth while tightly clutching her stomach. At this point I asked all the members to close the circle a bit and bring their chairs a little closer toward Shaniqua.

Asking victims of violence to close in on visible rage was a tall order, but they did it. I continued, "Since we know we didn't do anything to you since the last time we were together, we know you must be angry with or about someone or something else. I was wondering if maybe you wanted to tell people who care for you, about that."

Shaniqua rocked harder, like a soon to erupt volcano, and I signaled the group members to move closer. It was amazing to watch all of them push past their fears and begin to give and take strength from one another. By the time we had finished, group members were knee to knee with Shaniqua, and one member had her hand wrapped around Shaniqua's shoulders. I stood behind Shaniqua and gently rubbed her back. Shaniqua began to sob from her soul. She sobbed, she wailed, and she cried out, "Ain't never been nobody I can't scare away from me. Why you people look through me and care about me? Why you people care about me?" Then more gently and quietly, I heard her say. "Thank you for doin' that! Thank you!"

Week after week she continued to work hard. She seemed to be learning new and wonderful things about herself. She resumed her supervised visitation with her children, and we looked for a more appropriate apartment for her. I stepped in and advocated for her with landlords who were initially frightened when they did background checks on her. I wrote letters to her judge about all the therapeutic improvement I was seeing. She began to handle conflict and controversy with words instead of her teeth and fists. She discovered that words had more power than her rage. We celebrated when she came to group and told us that someone had made her so angry she normally would have "beat that person until they were dead. But I knew, I just knew, Trina ain't havin' none of that shit." I felt complimented that she could bring thoughts of me and some of my strengths with her into stressful situations, yet I also recognized her words as a red flag gently flapping in the breeze and pointed out to Shaniqua that she made those good choices because of her, not because of me.

At about the three-quarter mark of group, I became ill and was hospitalized for almost a month. The group went on hold, and when I returned, we needed to talk over how people felt about my sudden absence. Shaniqua was as sullen and moody as she had been the day she came to the group angry, months before. She bounced back and forth between crying and yelling. While doing both, she looked at me with tears rolling down her cheeks and said, "You was supposed to be here for me; you was supposed to sweep me up like a mother bird and carry me to places where I'm safe."

The red flag was no longer gently flapping; Shaniqua was shaking it in my face. I gently responded, "Shaniqua, I can't do that for you, and I never could. I'm just a mapmaker. I help you all make maps, and then you carry yourselves down the roads you choose. I believe in my heart that you are learning to take yourself to safe places. It's OK to feel angry or sad or scared because I wasn't here; that just means we miss people. But know in your heart that anything you do, you do! You have made all the improvement in your life, not me. By the way, I missed you too!" I felt more comfortable when Shaniqua said, "Yeah, I'm pretty strong now. I can make good choices."

The next day I was advised that Shaniqua had been arrested on an old bench warrant for assault. A piece of her past, before she had her new skills, was coming back to haunt her. Within two weeks she had been sentenced to serve six months in our county jail. I went to see her as much as I could. I tried to get there every week, but sometimes I couldn't. We talked about not slipping back, about holding onto the skills she had learned. She sent me journal pages, and I sent her letters. In them, we talked about feelings management and life, and children and all sorts of things. Some weeks I went to visit and found that she had been put in isolation for physical aggression against another inmate. Our goal was to hold on through the sentence and to try not to lose the skills she had developed. Incarceration eats a person up, and it was hard to keep the hope that she had found.

The six months ended, and Shaniqua called me when she was released. She was staying with another member of the group until she could find a place of her own. Out of jail for just one day, she was on the phone screaming about how this other group member had worn a pair of her sneakers while she was in jail and gotten them all muddy. Shaniqua was angry and threatening. I drove to the house; we sat, and I listened to her anger. She got up and marched around the room screaming, "She don't know, you don't know, what I had to do to get them sneakers. She got no business messing in my stuff. She make me so mad, she mess with me I'll beat her till she dead!"

I tried to validate her but also to get her to see that this group member did a lot for her while she was in jail. She stored her furniture and clothes; she moved the items; she sent Shaniqua underwear and toiletries that she needed; she was now providing her with shelter; and she had apologized and offered to replace the damaged sneakers. Not only could Shaniqua not go there with me, she looked at me again with tears streaming down her face and screamed, "Where was you, where was you all those times I was busting on somebody in that jail? Where was you when you was supposed to be telling me ways to not do that and end up in isolation? Where was you when I was crying in my cell at night? Where was you when them guards would mess with me and tell me stand up, sit down, walk on that side of the hall? Where was you when I would spit in their face? Where was you?"

I felt as if I was swallowing the red flag, and it was making me sick to my stomach. With each question I internally fluctuated between the literal and the defensive response. I remembered what a hassle it was to make visitation appointments, what a hassle it was when I got to the jail and the guards made me take off all my jewelry and then inspected my pockets. I remembered the day I forgot to bring a plastic bag and had to throw my jewelry in a metal locker. I watched my diamond earring fall between the cracks into the locker below me and had to wait until the person with that locker finished their visit so I could get my earring. Then I remember feeling like a schmuck for having diamond earrings to begin with. I reeled from her barrage of questions, but heard myself quietly respond, "I was home Shaniqua, I was home with my family, I was home where I am supposed to be."

There was silence for a while; then somehow we did some contracting for safety, and I left. My legs felt shaky as I walked to my car. I felt like I had lost a friend. I also felt that I had let go of someone falling, someone I was supposed to hang on to. Most of all, I felt sad and hurt and, at least for a moment, somewhat hopeless.

Shaniqua got on a bus to Florida the next day. She was going to go live with her Dad, and she intended to send a letter to the judge voluntarily terminating her rights with her kids. I got in my car, went home and had dinner with my family.

"I hope you will go out and let stories happen to you, and that you will work them, water them with your blood and tears and your laughter till they bloom, till you yourself burst into bloom. Then you will see what medicine they make and where and when it applies to them."

Clarissa Pinkola Estes
Women Who Run With the Wolves

Part Two

Witnessing the Sacred

Existing on The Edge

As therapists, we exist on the edge of another's reality
We circle around the pain in their story
Always watching for a space...

A sacred space...

Where we can invite them into their own wisdom
Where we can encourage them to see the gifts
Embedded in their trauma

When they enter this sacred space
They absorb a healing wisdom...
See new realities...
Move on in their lives

We stay behind
      Waiting...
      For new stories of pain
      New realities of yet another trauma
      To exist on the edge of...

Soul Fusion and Vicarious Trauma

In most people's lives there are few opportunities to witness miracles. We are grateful to have had countless opportunities to be awestruck by the resiliency of the human spirit. What has helped us to remain optimistic is that we have come not only to believe in miracles in therapy but to expect them. The stories in this section depict sacred moments of life. We have learned that we do not always have to be in charge of the therapy for these sacred moments to occur. We have come to believe that we can safely trust that what needs to happen will happen. Even as we listen to our clients' horror, we are searching for the miracle. As we swirl in and out of their words, we simultaneously intensely listen and search for the opportunity to infuse healing. This keeps us in love with our work. When one expects a miracle, even within horror, then the exchange of energy between the teller and the listener is less traumatic and more triumphant. It is difficult to put into words how honored we are to have witnessed the sacred in the following stories. The stories represent a brief moment in time, in which the therapist's soul (the listener) is fused with the soul of the client (the teller).

We present you with:

Winds of Change

Choosing Home

Trauma Rug

If I Could Only Smile

Twist of the Knife

The Story of Jacob

Winds of Change

Bonnie

Wind chimes are one of my favorite things, and I love the variety available these days. They can make so many different sounds depending on their size and shape. They can be cheap or expensive, but I don't know much about their cost because I never buy them for myself. People know I like them, so they give them to me as gifts. They give me great pleasure. I find them soothing and reassuring. They are a reminder of the dependability of Mother Nature. The sound of the chimes tells me she has sent wind to us again just as she sends sun and rain and snow and clouds.

There is a healing rhythm to nature that is important, especially for those who share their trauma stories with me. Their stories often have rhythms that are disturbing and out of sync with nature.

Susie's story is an example of how trauma can be triggered even by something the rest of the world sees as beautiful. Many people—her grandfather, his friends and even her own mother—abused Susie sexually. The abuse was frequent and continued for many years of her childhood. She came to me as an adult knowing that even though she had escaped from the abuse by running away at the age of 16, there was a residue of fear following her around even at the age of 43.

Susie was a big woman, strong and defensive. She walked with her head down and her hands curled into fists. She wore clothes of simple design, kept her hair short and wore no makeup. Only rarely would she wear earrings to a session or a pretty pin or necklace.

I grew very fond of Susie. I was in awe of her ability to survive to adulthood and to become a wife, a mother and a teacher. Judging by the stories of abuse she shared with me, by all rights she should have been dead or, at the very least, a drug addict or patient in a mental hospital. She was, indeed, a survivor.

We worked together for a long time. It was a delight to watch her work through her problems and deal with the paranoid feelings that had made her hypervigilant.

Susie grew in confidence and learned gradually to trust me and find some joy in her current life. However, one day, she came to see me because she felt she'd had a setback. She hurriedly entered the therapy room and sat quickly in a corner of the couch. She grabbed a pillow, and holding it tightly in front of her, she rocked her body and talked of her latest fear.

"We finally bought a new house. I am so proud to be able to own my own house. It shows how far I've come, since I grew up 'dirt poor' as they say. Everything was going well at first. This past weekend our friends helped us move in, and our kids are so excited. I must admit so am I. It's not a big house, but its well built and just right for us. I dared to be happy, and then it all fell apart."

I knew to remain silent and not ask questions of Susie. She would tell her story without any need for prodding from me. The silence deepened as Susie seemed to be gathering the strength to cope with her fear and to go on with her story.

"It fell apart that very first night in our new home. It was a beauti-ful summer night, so I left the window in our bedroom open for the warm breeze. My husband and I were very tired from a long day of moving, and we both fell asleep quickly. The next thing I knew I was sitting straight up in bed shaking and mumbling "no, no, no" over and over.

"I realized I was having a flashback of my father coming to my room at night when I was only five years old. But I don't know what triggered such a memory since I'd had a wonderful day and was so tired. I did my deep breathing exercise, lay back down and was just dozing off again when I heard it. I heard the sound that triggered my flashback. It was the sound of a wind chime. Our neighbor had one hanging on his back porch, which was near our bedroom window.

"I knew that sound. We had a wind chime when I was a child. It hung near my bedroom window then too. It is not a beautiful sound to me. It meant my Dad was home. He traveled a lot in the summer, but when he returned home on hot nights, he came to my room, opened the window and as the chime played, he fondled me and eventually fell asleep on top of me."

Susie continued, "Waking up abruptly the other night makes sense, but how do I live with this neighbor's wind chime now? Even with the window closed, I can hear it. Even though I understand that it's a trigger to the past, I still feel the fear in the present. What can I do? I'm hypervigilant again, and I can't sleep."

As I listened to Susie's story, I thought about my wind chime collection and felt sad that I was enjoying the chimes at perhaps the very same moment that Susie was fearing them.

I looked at her sitting and rocking and near tears. I wanted to comfort her, to tell her that it would be OK. I wanted to tell her, "That was then and this is now." I wanted to tell her how sorry I was that she had been deprived of enjoying even the rhythms of nature that the wind chimes symbolized.

However, I didn't say any of the above. I stood up and said, "Stay here for a moment. I'll be right back."

I left the therapy room and headed for the back door of my office, picking up a small step-stool on my way. I positioned the stool, climbed up on it and took down the wind chime I had recently hung next to the door as a welcome to all who entered the building.

I carried it carefully back to the therapy room, trying not to let it chime. I entered the room slowly, my heart in my throat, afraid that what I had in mind might not work. I feared that I could send Susie into a flashback and she would never forgive me.

As I entered the room, I asked for guidance from whomever it was that told me to trust my intuition! I sat down and gently laid the wind chime in my lap where it remained silent.

Susie stared at me, not with fear or anger, but with a look of confused curiosity. She cocked her head and looked first at me then at the chimes in my lap. Then she said, "What are you doing?"

I pushed past my own fear of hurting her and said, "Susie, do you know how much I admire you? How brave I think you are and how impressed I am with your ability to heal from such a tragic childhood?"

Susie just nodded her head in a "yes" motion.

"Well, I want you to enjoy your new house, your sense of accomplishment at being able to afford it and your joy in living in a comfortable setting. This is my housewarming gift to you.

"You see, I collect wind chimes. I collect them because I love their beautiful sounds, and they are a reminder to me that the wind always blows and the rain always rains and the sun always shines all in the rhythm of nature. I find that awareness is pleasant on good days and soothing and comforting on days that aren't so good.

"It's my wish for you that because this particular wind chime has been mine, when I give it to you, you will hear it chime the way I do. Whenever the wind blows and you hear it, you will think of all the healing you have done here in this place with me. It will then become a trigger for honoring your healing and your surviving to celebrate what you have become. That was then. This is now."

With that, I held the chime up and gently moved it so that we could hear the sound. It was as though there was a gentle breeze in the room.

We sat in silence for a while as I touched the chime to continue the sound. We were both mesmerized by it and needed no words to express our feelings.

Finally, Susie reached for the chimes and took them from me with a simple "Thank you." At that moment, I knew the winds had shifted, and the sound of the chimes announced a change in Susie's perception. Now, for both Susie and me, the sounds of those chimes served to remind us of hope and healing forever more.

Choosing Home

Trina

From the original phone contact, Ray had a tone of authority. He sounded like a man who got what he wanted, when he wanted. It wasn't aggression, more like persistence. It was difficult setting an appointment that worked with his tight schedule and mine. Thinking about it later, I realized that I was the one who did more giving and adjusting. I ended up making an appointment at a time when I was usually finished working and home for the evening. His persistence wore me down. I remember that even with his, "I get what I want attitude," there was also a quiet desperation. The silent desperation that I heard made me believe there was a need to set an appointment soon, even if it meant me flexing a bit.

The phone call provided very little information. Something odd had happened. In my desire to connect with him, I had not gathered as much information as usual. Questions that were second nature to me never got asked. For example, I didn't know how or by whom he was referred to me. I intentionally backed off asking him, "what prompted you to make the call to me?" or "what sort of things do you feel you need to talk about in therapy?"

I ask these standard screening questions so I can keep my client-base specific to trauma work, but I sensed that if I asked or if I pressed beyond his readiness, he would bolt.

It was after hours when he arrived for his session. The door automatically locked at 6 PM, so he needed to buzz my office. I went down and let him in. Through the full glass door, I saw a man in his early fifties. He had on black corduroy pants with a dress shirt that was open at the collar. His face and hands looked wonderfully tan against the shirt fabric. It is odd to say, but perhaps because of the tan, Ray exuded warmth, even though snow was falling lightly around him. When he entered the office, even before I offered my usual, "please have a seat wherever you are comfortable," he began moving some items off a wooden rocker that was very rarely used. He shifted the rocker closer to the chair that was obviously mine and positioned it about three feet in front of me.

I said, "Ray, I forgot to ask you how you were referred to my practice." He looked directly at me and said, " You came highly recommended. I have absolute trust in the person who recommended you. That person thinks the world of you; however, I'm not at liberty to say who it is."

This was the first of many comments that left Ray veiled in a cloak of mystery and secrecy. After a few exchanges like this, I finally needed to say, "Ray, I'm not sure I'm going to be able to provide you with a valuable service if you're not able to tell me why you are here." He seemed to soften a little and then quietly laughed. I now noticed that he was breathing more deeply. When he arrived, he was taking shallow half breaths. At this point, he told me how small the Boston medical community really is and asked if my proximity to the medical center meant that I was affiliated with the hospital. When I said I was not affiliated with the hospital, he relaxed and revealed that he was a physician and was very concerned about confidentiality. We discussed this to a level that Ray was comfortable with, and finally he revealed that he came because he was having relationship problems and wanted some objective insight. Ray had been married for twenty or so years. He reported that he and his wife had fallen out of love years earlier but had mutually agreed to stay together for their two sons. She had relationships on the side, and Ray did too. The sons were older now, so Ray and his wife would probably amicably divorce and split up marital assets. Ray would then be available for the woman he had seen exclusively for the last eight years.

As if he were doing a presentation for the American Medical Association, Ray went on to tell me what concerned him about his relationship with his girlfriend. He described a relationship that included great sex and similar interests. However, other aspects of the relationship drove him crazy. Words like "aspects" and "dynamics" and "interactions within the relationship" left me wondering whether he was having an intimate relationship with a cyborg or if he just operated from his head because his emotions were too vulnerable. Wonder never did me much good, so I asked him. He immediately fell silent, and his eyes opened wide enough to frame their blue with the clear white around them. He pressed back into the rocker, allowing him to move away from me without actually physically getting up and moving the chair. He stayed perched on his toes keeping the chair in the back rock position. Once again, I noticed he had stopped breathing, and once again I felt that if I pressed him, he might run.

At that moment I realized that he dealt with all people by getting them to run. He allowed them to pick up on his body language, and they instinctively backed off. If I was going to connect with this man, I needed to press, and I needed to start changing the rules. I began by taking a middle ground, suggesting that many of the doctors I had worked with were very bright individuals who spent years training themselves to interact intellectually rather than emotionally and spiritually. I defined this quality as common within the profession, not as a character defect within the man.

I suggested that when we accept this about ourselves, we can move forward and discover that what we teach ourselves to do professionally doesn't always necessarily work in more intimate nonprofessional relationships.

There was a pregnant silence, and I had an image of an emergency room setting in which a person is paddle shocked to restart their heart. I waited to see if my words were going to kick start Ray into breathing again or if, with the held breath he had left, he would roll up onto those perched toes and walk out of the room. The silence lasted a long minute. At last he rolled back down onto the balls of his feet and said, "that's exactly what Carol and I fight about. She says I don't connect with her, and I just don't get it."

Bravo, we had it! He had been able to verbalize that Carol wasn't wrong to feel that way, but there was something within himself that he "just didn't get." He went on to say that he was having vague recollections of his wife saying similar things years ago, before they went their separate ways.

It was a calculated risk when I said, "So what are you afraid of Ray?" Followed by, "We're out of time, but why don't you think about that question for next time."

To suggest fear to this "I get what I want, I'm in control" man, was a risk, but he had connected with me and was now at least intellectually intrigued by what I was saying.

He suggested, "Well I know I'm your last client tonight. No one is waiting, and I'll pay you the extra, so we can just keep going." My silent mantra was playing in my head, "You've got to change his rules; you've got to change his rules."

As I stood up, I simply said, "Not tonight Ray, I'm not able to do that. Let's set another appointment." He clearly did not like not getting his way, but he accepted it and readied himself to leave.

I saw Ray two weeks later. He seemed less tan and definitely more tired. He reported having had trouble sleeping since his last appointment. He also reported having an argument with his girlfriend, Carol, and even one with his wife. He was particularly distressed about the fight with his wife.

He said, "There hasn't been anything passionate enough to fight over in that relationship for fifteen years." I questioned why he didn't give me a call about the sleep disturbances, but he brushed it off with an "I can handle it myself "answer.

I offered, "Maybe the fear question we ended with was working on you subconsciously?" He retorted, "I really didn't give that much thought. As a matter of fact, I don't even understand why you would make such a statement."

He went on to tell me why fear isn't an issue for him. I learned that he was not only a physician, he was a neurosurgeon. He let me know that he was "made of money." The long and the short of it was that he perceived himself as at the top of his game and had nothing to be afraid of. If it didn't work out with Carol, he'd find somebody else.

I suggested that "understanding" fear was precisely the problem. Understanding is an intellectual system, but fear is an emotional event. Trying to force a feeling into an intellectual medium would probably keep a person up nights. This seemed intriguing to Ray. By now he was perspiring, and I asked if he would like me to turn the heat down a bit. He seemed somewhat panicked, his breathing was shallow and irregular, and his eyes shifted and fixated. He clearly was remembering something that was not about the here and now in my office.

I found myself asking, "Where are you right now Ray? What are you seeing?"

He responded by saying, "Oh I was just thinking about something that I hadn't thought of for a while. I do remember one time I was scared, but I really haven't been scared since then.

I was in Vietnam, and my platoon had just been hit pretty hard by the Viet Cong. We had all scattered in a million different directions, and there were napalm fires burning all around us. The smell was awful, and as I ran it became harder and harder to breathe. The smoke was burning the hairs in my nose, and my lungs felt really hot. I just ran and ran. I thought I knew how to get to the pick-up spot. Through the smoke I couldn't see them, but I could hear the rescue choppers, and I ran in the direction of the chopper noise. But the other noise, the noise of Vietnamese shouting, and the sound of them running behind me, was scaring me. They were right behind me, chasing me—or it at least seemed like they were chasing just me. They were probably chasing all of us who were left. Then the sound of their voices shifted, and the sound of their running was in another direction. I knew they were chasing someone else from my platoon. I could hear their voices escalate. They got louder and all seemed to be frantically talking together, and then I heard a single shot.

I knew they had found one of us, and they all encouraged each other to "shoot him, shoot him." One of my friends was dead, and I began to run harder. I was out of breath and I fell. At ground level, under the smoke in front of me, was Taylor. Taylor was hurt really bad, and I could see a gaping hole in his chest. I didn't think that that much blood could come out of anyone. Taylor was crying and telling me, "I want to go home Ray. I want to go home!"

I told him, "I know man, I know. The choppers are just ahead I'll get you there." I tried to lift him; we moved a foot and we both fell. I picked him up again, and this time barely got him off the ground. I began to drag him by his shirt, and he screamed in excruciating pain. He pulled me down on top of him; he was clutching my shirt, holding me close to his face as he said, "I want to go home Ray. Send me home Ray." I jumped up out of his reach and just stared at him.

He said, "I'm scared man. I can't go further, and I'm gonna die; I know I'm gonna die, Don't let the Cong get me first. Please Ray, I'm begging you. Send me home. Please Ray, I want to go home!"

I could hear the choppers; I could hear the enemy shifting back towards us. I could hear Taylor who now was gasping desperately for air.

At this point Ray was sobbing, and I sat silent and frozen, mesmerized by the man before me. I feared that any shift in my posture or my breathing would break the spell of release that Ray had wandered into.

"'Go home Taylor. Go home man!' I shot him one time in his left temple, and then I ran and ran and ran."

That session is frozen in my brain, and in my heart. There are times when people share their pain that the very environment of the room changes. It's as though the molecular structure of the furniture that holds you knows to just quietly listen and support your weight. It's as though the putrid smell of the napalm burns the listener's throat as well as the teller's. The therapeutic moment becomes frozen, suspended in the thick jungle air that was once your office. It is suspended by a heavy awareness that no moment from then on to infinity, can ever be wrapped in a formerly naïve unawareness. It is as though the tears that rolled off Ray's face were dropping onto my own heart, making a healing/hurting ping sound as they hit.

Ray went on to tell me that he had never told another human being that story—a story that began over thirty years ago. Before he told it, he had never understood why he'd had such a tremendous drive to become a doctor, a surgeon, a healer. He never knew why medical school was a must for him. He never knew why he was unlike the other interns and residents he went to school with—he had never been fatigued, not once, never.

He could only see the end, the end when he became the neurosurgeon, when he got to put people's brains back together after auto accidents or brain tumors or aneurysms. He never realized that he was petrified that if he got close to anyone, they would see right through him. They would see what he believed was his evil core—a core that was too ugly for the human eye to see, the human heart to embrace.

Ray did not remain in therapy for long. We worked together for three or four months. We worked long enough for him to realize that the running he did in Viet Nam had never really stopped. We worked long enough for him to take Taylor's watch, which was buried in a trunk in his attic, to the wall in Washington, where he left it beneath Taylor's name. We worked long enough for Ray to realize that he had really good sex with Carol, and that that was about it. He learned that sex had been a way for him to release a lot of pain for a long time. We worked long enough for him to realize that sex was a sideways release of his need to express something, somehow. We worked long enough for him to realize that he had more with his wife than he had with Carol and long enough to refer them both to a marriage counselor because choosing home was what they both wanted.

I guess we all choose home in some way, albeit differently. Taylor chose home. Ray and his wife chose home. For me, visiting in people's souls and sacred moments feels like home, but really I'm just visiting. I left that memorable session with Ray and got to my real home late. The youngest of my boys was about ten at the time and had already gone to bed. I stood in his doorway watching him sleep and hoping. I was hoping that he would never have to leave home, but I knew that he would. Yet I trusted that like others and like me he would choose to find his way back home.

Trauma Rug

Bonnie

It wasn't like I hadn't heard terribly sad stories before, but this woman had suffered such severe sexual trauma as a child, I wondered how she was able to sit in front of me and tell me story after story of the horrors she had been through.

She spoke softly and looked down at her lap as she told me of her mother torturing her and her father sharing her sexually with other men. She described scene after scene of trauma. Her voice would tremble, and sometimes she stopped speaking all together and seemed to be gathering some miraculous inner strength, which would quietly renew her courage to continue her stories.

She always sat so still facing away from me. She seldom even glanced at me to see if I was still next to her on the couch where she had requested that I sit.

Session after session she talked with very few tears, but she continued to tremble as though the tears were traveling throughout her body searching for a way out. She never missed a session and continued to ask me to push her to tell more—knowing that the telling was a way to break through her shame and get to the deep hurt and agony waiting to be released.

Each session started with a hug and talk of her daily struggles. She was a teacher with a compassion for her students beyond what was required of her. Then she would say, "Do you want to go there?" My response would always be yes, and she got me to promise that I would push the telling of these stories. When she had told as much as she dared at that point in her healing, she would say, "Have you had enough?"

When I responded, "Have you had enough?" she would hang her head even lower and cry slowly. Eventually she'd stand up, still with her head down, and go to the door. She'd take a deep breath and turn to go, but only after we hugged.

As the stories continued to be released, she began to vary her routine. She would bring me coffee, and we would chat like two old friends before getting to the "push" part of her session.

She also would write to me between sessions to share how our work was healing for her and how what we did together was changing her daily life. She became eager to tell me about the new joys she was finding in her life—such joys as walking the beach with her head held high, laughing with friends without fear, playing with her children in a much freer way than before the telling of her story.

As the sessions progressed, she began to raise her head, and we looked at each other as she integrated a new awareness that came to her during the session. Finally, the day came when she felt she could leave therapy, go out into the world, and practice her newfound freedom. I was proud of her and impressed with her courage and resiliency.

At what was to be her last session of therapy, she spoke to me of the rug. In front of the couch we always sat on together, I had placed a throw rug. She shared with me on that last day that she had always focused on that rug as she told her stories of horror.

Now at this, the last session, she explained that she did this because she believed she was pouring her childhood abuse stories into that rug. She wanted to believe this was a way to leave the stories here so she would be released from carrying them around with her in her current life. She also felt that pouring such horrors into this rug was safer than sharing them with me. She didn't want to pour them into me. She worried about me carrying these stories inside of me forever, and she knew what that felt like. She cared about me too much to burden me with such trauma.

I told her how wise she was to find a way to contain those stories that was both safe for her and protective of me. As the session ended, she stood and as usual asked for a hug. We stood in our embrace and she said she wanted to ask me one more thing.

"Anything," I said, hoping I could answer a question of one with so much wisdom. She said, "May I take that rug home and wash it of all its trauma?" I caught my breath and at that moment realized what a wonderful idea that was. I eagerly rolled up the rug and handed it to her. We walked out of my office, down the hall together and out to her car. We both agreed that we somehow felt lighter and freer as we shared how the washing of the rug would release the pain and suffering into the universe where it would dissipate and be gone.

As I waved goodbye to her, I wondered, "Whose healing was that anyway?"

If I Could Only Smile

Trina

My first conversation with Robert was over the phone. When he began speaking, I couldn't tell whether he had a foreign accent or some sort of physical disability. His speech was hard to understand, yet I found that if I closed my eyes, I could "see" the words better than I could actually hear them. It got easier as the call went on, and I established that he was referred by his primary doctor because he was feeling very depressed.

The day of his appointment I went to the waiting room to meet him and found him reading a magazine. He appeared to be in his late 50s or early 60s and at least six feet tall. From my angle of approach, he didn't look foreign. As he stood to greet me, he turned to shake my hand and exposed the right side of his face for the first time. It was severely scarred; it looked as if the top half of his cheek had been pulled as tight as possible and fastened to the lower half, leaving a deep indentation where the two halves met. His mouth had been pulled very tightly toward the side of his face. As I remembered our phone call, it became apparent to me that this was the reason behind the difficulty I had understanding him.

I soon learned that Robert was actually in his early 70s. His youthful appearance testified to a man who had stayed active and vibrant. Robert had served on the town board of his little hamlet for years. He was a former teacher who knew everyone, having taught a parent or child or both for almost every family in town.

About a year and a half prior to our meeting, Robert was diagnosed with mouth cancer. Today he was free from the spread of the ravaging disease; however his freedom came with the removal of half of his tongue and a great deal of his cheek and neck. Surgery was over as either the doctors had done all the reconstruction they could do, or Robert had had enough. He now went to a speech therapist three times a week.

The more time I spent with Robert, the easier his speech was to understand. Depression was not a difficult diagnosis to make. This man's entire life was about being a speaker. He had used his education and intellect, through his words, as an educator and as a town spokesperson. Surgery and illness had turned topsy-turvy his sense of who he was now and what he could be for the rest of his days. When words became difficult to both deliver and understand, Robert began to question whether he had any worth.

As he talked, he actually broke into a sweat and asked if I could understand him. Once he felt comfortable that I understood him, he talked openly and honestly about how the disease had affected him. There was an easy-going rhythm to our sessions, and it often felt like I was meeting an old friend for coffee and a visit.

He must have had that same, "like I've known you forever" feeling, because one day, in the course of a story, he spontaneously said, "Yeah, when they told me what the surgery was going to be like, it was like the day of the slap. I knew the same thing the day of the slap that I knew the day they told me about the surgery." When I asked what that was that he knew, Robert softly and rather meekly responded, "Oh you just know in your bones that life is just never going to be the same or never even be good again."

As we began to talk more deeply, Robert revealed that the slap that set up the rest of Robert's life to be "never even good again" was delivered when Robert was six years old some 70 years earlier. This proud and gentle man wept when he told me about the day he was walking his sister home. Robert was two years older than his sister, and he had been entrusted with walking her from the bakery back home. Mom and Dad had gone ahead after the Sunday service, allowing Robert to go in, buy the bread and walk the short block back home. I am often amazed at the way in which people remember things from their past. It's as if their present substance silently floats out of the room and is replaced with the child they are remembering. Before me I saw a perfectly intact little boy. In my mind's eye, the surgical ravages on Robert's face were transformed, replaced with the smooth sun-tanned skin of a six-year-old. As he remembered how proud he was at having received such a grownup assignment, his eyes glistened with pride and excitement. He recounted how he felt and felt again for the quarter in his pants pocket. He was unsure which part of the assignment made him feel more responsible. He had been entrusted with his little sister, whom he adored. With one hand, he squeezed her hand to be sure he had a good hold on her and also to be sure that the moment was real. With the other hand he confirmed that the quarter was safe in his pocket; sure that it was more money than anyone had ever been entrusted with.

He watched his parents get all the way to the front gate and go into the house before he entered the bakery, having decided that only when they entered the house would he actually be on his grown up assignment. No one was watching him from around the corner; he was officially responsible and in charge.

The bakery bell on the back of the door announced their arrival to Mr. Woodson, the bakery owner. Robert talked about hearing the bell and remembering the sound as if it announced, "Mr. Robert Knight, the big boy, has arrived. Step to it; he would like a loaf of fresh-baked bread."

He remembered that Mr. Woodson must have heard the bell say that too because he looked down at Robert and his sister and said, "Well good morning Mr. Knight. Lovely Sunday morning isn't it?

I have fresh loaves just out of the oven, might I get you one?"

Robert remembered feeling as if he would fall over. Being called Mr. Knight played over and over in his head. Robert gave a bit of a chuckle and smiled as he related this 70-year-old story.

He told me, "I can't even remember if I told him, 'yes, please,' or not. I just remember being Mr. Knight and somehow the quarter coming out of my pocket, the bread coming into my arms and the bakery bell, as the door closed behind me, announcing to the pedestrians on the street, 'Here comes Robert-Knight-Big-Boy.'"

As he approached the gate at his front walk, his Dad was coming out of the house. Robert could barely wait to hand him the bread. Somehow the transfer would make the mission complete. Robert's father approached with the same excitement. They got to the gate at the same moment, and Robert was amazed as his father snatched him up by his shirt and slapped him as hard as he could across his face. He remembered seeing the bread float out his arms.

Robert said to me, "I remember my father's words sounded distorted and his face was ugly with rage. He screamed at me, 'How could you not watch Lily? What's the matter with you boy, are you stupid? Why did your sister get home without you? How many times did I tell you to hold her hand?'"

There before me was a 70-year-old man, crying the tears of a six-year-old boy. Tears rolled gently down the left side of Robert's face. Although there were tears in his right eye, they came down his cheek and got lost in the scar that pieced the two halves of his face together. I remember thinking that they got lost as they had for the past 70 years. They had been lost from easily retrievable memory until one day when he heard about a surgery that would change his life. On that day, he felt like it was "the day of the slap."

In the course of the next couple of months, Robert told me lots of stories about being his father's son. We didn't talk much about the cancer or his current depression. We talked a lot about his dad's alcoholism, his dad's explosive temper, the Christmas his dad threw the Christmas tree through the front picture window and the night they got the call from the sheriff late in the night.

Robert wasn't sure if he became a man that night, the night his Dad wrapped his car around the tree and was killed, or if he became a man the day when he saw the warm loaf of bread fly out of his grasp. We talked a lot about the difference between transitions into manhood versus the theft of innocence. By midNovember, Robert was off his antidepressant and back at town board meetings. He looked forward to attending an awards dinner at which he was to be the recipient of his town's lifetime achievement award.

One day in my office, Robert grinned, as best he could, about the acceptance speech he had written. He was genuinely grateful when he said, "When I started coming here, I was afraid to talk to anyone, even my wife. I was afraid no one could understand me. Now I'm getting ready to make a speech, with lots and lots of people looking at me. I guess I've been worrying about the wrong kind of understanding. It seems like you understood me just fine." The moment passed and we began talking about the holidays.

I was taken a bit off guard when Robert announced that he had always hated the holidays. With all the things he had overcome and survived as a result of being raised in his household, the one that remained the most challenging was the holidays. Year after year, he was grumpy and irritable. He always had a "bah, humbug" attitude but felt tremendously guilty about that.

Robert and his wife married late in life. They had one daughter, now in her early 30s, who was born with developmental disabilities and had been in a wheelchair all her life. She lived with them and was totally dependent on them. As hard as Robert tried, he couldn't shake the ghosts that haunted him during the holidays.

He felt his daughter's experience with the holidays was, in some ways, as bad as his had been, and he could never be a good enough dad during this time of year.

A couple of weeks later, I left for an extended holiday in Chicago. Robert and I ended our sessions the week before I left. He had attained the goals he had set for our work together.

As I wandered in and out of shops on Chicago's Magnificent Mile, I stumbled into a cozy bookstore, which was inviting and offered warm cider. On the promotional table, I found a Caldecott Award winning children's book called *The Polar Express.* Beside the hard-bound book lay a narrated tape, on which William Hurt read the story. I took the sample package into a listening room and thumbed through the book, gazing at the illustrations, as William Hurt's strong, soft voice walked me through this beautiful story about Christmas and believing. Although it was somewhat expensive, and although I was not in the habit of buying my clients holiday presents, I purchased it purely with Robert in mind.

The girl at the counter asked if I wanted the book wrapped and shipped, but I declined because I wanted to wrap it myself. I remembered the elaborate wrapping we had on presents from my grandmother. The present itself may simply have been a pair of hand-knit socks, but the foil wrapping with a decorative pin or handmade toy or decoration on top, made it very special. Gramma's presents were like boxes of magic. They were elaborate labors of love, which made other presents under the tree seem lifeless. Although I knew that it would be impossible for Robert to feel the way I did with my grandmother, I wanted very much for Robert's present to at least look like mine of old. I bought a pretty red foil wrap and added a green satin flat ribbon with a white dove poised at its center. A sprig of red holly berries and a single Christmas bell gently hung from the dove's beak. The next day I headed off to the post office and shipped Robert's present. The card read, "Robert, I found this story about magic and believing. For some reason it reminded me of you. May you and your family have the happiest of holidays."

When I returned to my office after the New Year holiday, a card awaited me.

Trina,

I can't thank you enough for the present. Although the man on the tape is very eloquent, I have taken to reading the story aloud myself to my daughter and my wife. They seem to like it best when I read it. The first time I read it out loud, I was propped up beside my daughter on her bed. It was as though I was tucking her in, like so many years ago. There is no other word to describe her face as I read, other than sheer delight.

I remember when we first started working together, one of my complaints was that my face was so distorted that I couldn't smile. It seemed like no matter how I tried to contort my face, it never quite looked like a smile. I distinctly remember saying, "If I could only smile!"

I just want to let you know, seeing my daughter that night, and realizing that I was the source of her happiness… Well, let me just say, my face hasn't changed much, but I felt what it feels like to smile from my soul.

Thank you,
Robert

I knew in that moment what it felt like too.

Twist of the Knife

Bonnie

My thoughts were racing. This man scared me. He appeared agitated and hypervigilant, as though he didn't want to be here. I felt that if I spoke or even moved in a way that upset him, he would jump at me or become angry and leave.

Although George was tall and well-built, he had an unkempt appearance and a strange smell—like dried sweat mixed with dust. His unshaven face was swarthy with deep dark circles under his eyes. His hands were always moving through his hair or along his thighs as he wiggled in his seat.

I watched those hands and studied his appearance, my internal tension beginning to match his obvious distress. Trying very hard not to show my fear, I suddenly realized that he had been talking, and I hadn't heard what he said. I felt like I was preparing myself to be self-protective rather than attempting to be open and receptive to his pain.

"I'm here because my wife will leave me if I don't do something about how I'm acting. I get angry with her when she doesn't understand. (I wondered how angry as my fear mounted.) I want to hit her and scream at her. I want her to see what's happening to me. She just doesn't get it." He talked fast, pounding his fist on his thigh and rocking in his seat as he spoke.

I remained quiet, hoping that telling me his story would release some of his pent-up anger. I simply asked, "What is it that she doesn't get?"

The dam burst! He spoke in loud, rapid outbursts, his voice filled with rage. He intensified his anger by pounding one fist against the other as he paced across the room and back.

"I'm being persecuted by the federal government! They are watching me all the time. They forced me to be late for work and not get the work done so I got fired. They made my children hate me, so they avoid me now. My wife is starting to avoid me too, but nobody understands. I'm trying to escape the government watching me. I have shades on all my windows. I lock doors as I go in and out of rooms in my own house. If I go out, I drive fast and take detours and shortcuts to get where I need to go just in case they are following me. I had to do that to get here today. I don't want to be here either. How do I know you aren't part of the government and they aren't going to come in that door and grab me at any minute?"

With that, he stood up, went to the door and examined it, looking for a lock. My heart raced. The idea of being locked in with this guy was very frightening. I swallowed, took a deep breath and said, "The door doesn't lock. It's been broken for years."

He looked at me from across the room, came over, sat down right in front of me and asked, "How do I know you won't turn me in?"

I thought that was a good question, based on his belief system, so I looked him in the eye and said, "Simply because I'm not out to get you, and I wouldn't know how to turn you in even if I wanted to."

He dropped his eyes and sat quietly for a moment—the first quiet moment since he entered the room. His stillness made me brave. I let out a breath I didn't know I'd been holding and said, "Tell me how this all happened. Start at the beginning."

In a quiet voice, he began to share his pain of isolation, his fears of being followed and his anger at feeling helpless. I felt myself regain my composure, my own body letting go of the tension produced by my fear of this man's rage.

His story was a classic one. He was truly paranoid. Everything scared him—the look of a driver on the road next to him, the sound of a siren in the distance, the stories on the nightly news. He believed that all these things were attempts by the federal government to capture him. His pain was intense, and he shared with me how he had isolated himself as a way of coping with his fears.

"I make it a point to be alone as much as possible. I never answer the phone. I don't go the door if I have visitors. I feel at times that I don't even want my wife around me. I actually feel relieved when she avoids me."

He paused for a moment, and I hoped he was feeling better for having told me about his fears, but suddenly he escalated again. He said in a loud clear voice, looking right at me with sad eyes, "Oh hell, I'm tired. Turn me in."

He held out his hands in front of me in a gesture that looked like he was asking me to handcuff him. I was speechless and suddenly felt an overwhelming sense of compassion for this man.

When I didn't respond in any way, his anger escalated again. He stood up, paced again and then abruptly left the room, saying over and over, "I knew you couldn't help me. I knew it. You can't help me. Nobody can!"

After he left, my first reaction was one of relief followed quickly by guilt that I would feel relief! "Good riddance," I thought and then immediately felt ashamed of myself. My next reaction was to go to my diagnostic manual and look up paranoid ideation. I wanted to help but I didn't know how. The manual is really no help except for the advice that encouraged "medication and keep under constant supervision."

I went to the phone and called his wife. Charlotte is a loyal, patient woman, who has tried to help her husband, but she told me she was feeling as helpless as he was. As she started to cry on the phone, she said, "I worked so hard to get him to come and see you. I guess I thought you could perform some miracle."

I told her that in my work, I always expect miracles but I don't perform them. We made a plan for me to see George again—this time with her in the session also.

The following week, miracles did begin to happen. George returned with Charlotte and seemed much calmer and less angry. He and Charlotte sat together on the couch and held hands as they jointly told about what their lives had been like lately.

Charlotte said to me, "George is back on his medication now, and we both know that makes him feel so much better. Right George?"

"Yes," responded George, "But I know I can get off this damn stuff once I get back on track with my life. I don't plan to stay on this forever."

Charlotte and I both tried to convince him that staying on meds was really the best thing for him, maybe even forever.

I said, "You appear so different. You are calmer, less fearful and more communicative. I think the medicine is bringing out the best in you. I feel like I am now getting to know the real you under all that anger and fear. Thank you for coming back to see me."

George looked me right in the eye and said in a clear calm voice, "Tell me the truth. Were you afraid of me last time I was here?"

I hesitated, but not long. I knew I had to be honest with him because that is my style. "Yes," I said trying to sound strong and confident about what I was saying, "I was very afraid of you. You were so full of rage about so many things. I feared that I would be added to the list of people you were angry at."

Continuing to practice honesty, I said, "George, I was relieved at first when you left in such a hurry. My first thought was 'Good riddance!' But you know what? That feeling of relief didn't last long. I began almost immediately to feel sad. I was sad that you had to live with the doors locked, the blinds pulled, isolated and alone. Then I felt a sense of awe when I realized what it must have taken to get yourself to my office. How courageous you are. You must have had a sense of hope or you never would have made that first appointment or this one for that matter. I admire you George, and I would like to be your therapist if you'll let me."

By this time, Charlotte was quietly crying, playing with her hands in her lap sitting in a far corner of the couch. We were all silent for a long time.

George was the first to speak: "Nobody ever admired me," he said quietly, and then he actually smiled as he sat back on the couch and moved closer to Charlotte handing her a tissue with a gentleness that seemed the antithesis of his nature.

The energy exchange among us slowed down, and I prepared to end the session. I commented, "I think we are on the right track. As I watch you two together now, I feel the bond that will help you through this George."

George said nothing but nodded and left the room. Charlotte lingered to schedule another appointment.

After they left, I wondered if I could ever be as loyal as Charlotte to a person like Ray. The sessions went along smoothly from that point on. I met with George and Charlotte regularly and supported his staying on medication. We developed strategies for coping with the pressures he felt in his life.

All seemed to be going well. George was still leery of having too many people around him, and he still didn't like to come out of the house too often. He stayed on his medication reluctantly but seemed to know it was for the best.

After about six months of these sessions, George requested a vacation from therapy. We talked about how he could take care of himself, and he agreed to come back if he or Charlotte felt he needed to. I said with a smile, "My door will always be open. Remember that first day when I told you my lock doesn't work?"

I had mixed feelings about his mental health, but I knew he needed to try life on his own much as we all do at some points in our lives. I didn't feel he really had come to grips with his problem as a mental illness, and I worried that if he ever went off his meds he would return to that extreme paranoia and the rage that went with it. Of course, that is exactly what happened.

I was working on paperwork late one night and was alone in the office when George quite literally burst in on me as I sat at my desk. Although it was the middle of winter with the temperature in the 20s and snow falling outside, he stood in front of me stripped to the waist, bare-chested and shoeless with a look of intense terror in his eyes.

The cold chill that ran down my spine contrasted with the heat he radiated as he stood in front of me poised like a fighter with his legs apart, knees bent and arms spread wide.

He said in a very loud anxiety-filled voice, "I knew I'd find you here. I knew you would be waiting for me!"

At that moment, I felt that my worst fears had materialized before my eyes. I had become part of his paranoia, and he truly believed that I, like everyone else, was out to get him. I knew I was alone in the building and would have to find a creative way to get help for him (and for me).

I asked him to sit down and was relieved when he did. I said, "Are you cold?"

He said, "No. Why?"

I continued, "You don't have any shoes or coat?" He looked down at his bare feet and exposed chest then said with a tremble in his voice, "I'm so warm and my feet felt so tight in my shoes. I feel better this way."

He studied me. The silence was not reassuring to me. I waited. He waited. Neither of us moved for a long time, sitting there across from each other in an empty building, late at night, each wrapped in our own fears about what could happen next.

My mind raced as I explored my options. "How can I help? What should I do? Will he hurt me? Is he as scared as I am? Will he explode any minute?" I didn't know what to do.

George solved that problem for me when he suddenly stood up and came toward me as I sat at my desk. I was preparing to scream, to dodge and run past him. It was at that intensely fearful moment that I saw he had a knife in his outstretched hand. My fear escalated, and I put my hands up in a position of surrender.

He laughed a hideous laugh but immediately became serious and said in a quiet almost tender voice, "Hey don't be scared. I'm not going to hurt you. I'm here because you told me once you admired me for being so brave. I never forgot that, and right here, right this minute, I don't know anyone else who admires me. I'm pretty low, and I could use this knife on myself because I don't want to live any longer. I'm here because I want to give you this knife. I need you to stop me from killing myself. I need you to help me."

With that, he threw the knife on my desk, fell to his knees, put his hands over his face and began to wail like a wild animal. My fear dissipated with that sound (and the fact that the knife was on my desk). I got down on the floor next to him and rocked him, taking softly all the time about still admiring him and wanting to help him. He knew he was off his meds and agreed to get back on them.

I called Charlotte and within 30 minutes, she and two crisis counselors transported him to the hospital, treating him with the respect and dignity he deserved.

How did I help? It seems simple now as I look back on it. I, like Charlotte, found I could be loyal even to a person who was unpredictable and frightening. Of course, because of working with George, I certainly increased my respect for psychotropic mediations. But even more than that, I had admiration for the resiliency of the human spirit that hangs onto hope at all costs.

The Story of Jacob

Trina

ris was 38. She had five children from three different husbands. Her present husband was abusive and controlled her physically, financially and spiritually. Iris had made three serious suicide attempts in her lifetime. She had established a pattern in which she used heroin when she became very depressed. For many years, she overdosed and was hospitalized shortly before the holidays. By springtime she would have a new lease on life, but the cycle would start all over again. Iris had multiple diagnoses. She had done chemical dependency work, but until she joined my group, she had never done any therapeutic work around being an adult survivor of childhood incest at the hands of her pastor father.

Iris had struggled with the group process for the last several weeks. She worked openly and diligently in the beginning weeks as we did some preliminary bonding work. She allowed herself to connect with the other members of the group, and she lapped up psychoeducation material, seeing how it fit into her life experience. When we did the work around identifying coping mechanisms, it was as if flash bulbs were going off in rapid succession, enlightening how she had become the person she thought she was.

As we introduced the concept of breaking the secret, we watched her begin to close down. The radiance that had emerged began to pale a little, and bricks and mortar were brought into group with her on a weekly basis. Iris slathered on extra mortar as she placed her final brick and declared, "I cannot and will not do this exercise!"

She didn't seem relieved when we told her that she did not have to do it. We reiterated that our group is called CHOICES and that she always had a choice to do or not do any activity that was being offered. Two other members had shared their stories on consecutive weeks. Including Iris, there were three more to go. During their sharing Iris often gently cried, or we saw her fists tighten in anger. Her ability to identify with, empathize, and offer compassion to her fellow group members was intact, yet at the end of every group she would bring one of us aside and repeat, "I can't do this and I won't do this."

The format used by the other members telling their stories didn't fluctuate much. Most of them began with a chronology of sorts and ultimately got to a place in which we could identify initial trauma and begin to look at how messages were internalized or cognitive schemas were developed as a result of that trauma. We had begun this particular group in early September; it was now late October. On this October day, we brought in cider and donuts. Group members got their snack and visited a bit before we began. Iris arrived a bit later than usual, yet still on time. She came into the group room already speaking as she crossed through the doorway.

She forcefully said to all of us, "If I am going to do this, I have to do it now, or I'll never be willing again."

The other members rose to the occasion, encouraging her and expressing gratitude that she felt safe enough with them to share such an important piece of her history. I have heard many stories of incest, abuse, and betrayal, each of them touching me in a solemn and sacred way, but Iris's story reduced me to tears.

Iris began to read from a neatly folded paper that she took from her purse:

Dear Jacob,

It has been such a long time since I've spoken to
you, but I never ever for one second have forgotten
you. Of all the people in my life, you were always
there for me, and like the rock that you were, you
were constant, strong and dependable. No matter
what they did to me, I could always reach out to
you and touch you; you would hold my hand.
Such comfort I got from your touch, even though
your touch was cold and rough. I knew it was just
that you were an old man and your hands and
fingers had gotten bony and rough from the hard
and honest work that I knew you must have done
all your life. You knew Papa was a minister; it was
never uncommon on those Saturdays to see him
walking with me through the cemetery. It seemed
appropriate that he was going and praying over
the graves of his parishioners. We would wind our
way through, and the closer we got the colder and
more dead inside I would become. I knew it was
pointless to show my fear, and I had to concentrate
so hard on not throwing up. While I laid on that
mound of dirt, while my Papa put his penis in and
out of me, I reached out to you, my face always
turned in your direction. And even though my eyes
were shut as tight as I could shut them, my fingers
would trace the J, then the A, then C, O, B of your
name. I knew by feel every letter, bump and crack
on your tombstone. On that Saturday, the most
horrible one, I was not only dead inside and sick to
my stomach, I was also so cold. It was too cold for
Halloween; everyone was talking about how early
it had snowed. We never had snow for Halloween
before. The only comfort I had as we walked that
winding path was that you would be there as al-

ways to keep me warm. The snow was freezing on my bottom. I reached up as I always did to touch your name, but the snow had filled in all the places where your name was carved. I couldn't touch you or reach you, and I became so terrified that I had to open my eyes. I looked in your direction but couldn't see you there to be with me. On this day Papa's brother and his grownup son were there to rape me too. They had probably been there before, but I never had to know because I was with you. But today I did know, and in the knowing I began to cry. As I cried the snow magically began to melt away from your stone, and once again I could close my eyes and reach out and trace,

JACOB STRUTT

1902-1965

LOVING HUSBAND AND FATHER

Today is All Souls Day again, but now it is some 29 years later. Today seemed like the perfect day to let other living souls hold my hand and comfort me and let you rest in peace. Maybe this year when winter comes and the snow makes me feel so terrified, I won't have to shoot my veins with drugs that help make the terror go away. I love you Jacob.

Love,
Iris

"Stories have to be told
or they die, and when they die,
we can't remember who we are
or why we are here."

Sue Monk Kidd
The Secret Life of Bees

Part Three

Making A Difference

I Stand In a Forest Differently

If I had known then,
What I know now,
I would have heard the forest
Speak to me.

If I could feel then,
What I feel now,
I would have allowed the forest
To nurture me.

Even though from the time I was small,
It was always grand with majesty,
The forest was just my playground,
I didn't see its mystery.

That seems like only yesterday,
A moment, a second, a morsel of time.
So many lives have entered my world
That the forest has changed, or is it me?

I do know now,
What I didn't know then,
I can hear now,
What I couldn't hear then.

It is the stories I hear in the rustling leaves.
I see the faces of the tellers in the swirling wind.
The warmth of their healing in the rays of the sun,
The pain of their losses in the dampness of
    shadows.

My life has changed when I visit the forest,
No longer alone to play, but joining with the leaves
    and the wind.
I am now honored when the forest speaks,
For I stand in a forest differently.

How Finding Meaning in Our Work Relieves Vicarious Trauma

It feels tremendously good, as therapists and as people, to have been agents of change. There is no other work we can imagine doing that would allow us to feel as good about ourselves as this work. The stories in this section validate for us that when tellers and listeners join together there is potential for tremendous change. Knowing that we are making a difference is an antidote to vicarious trauma. Even if we at times take home nightmares or sometimes feel compassion fatigue, we can replenish ourselves by remembering that we are making a difference. Difference comes in the form of a life change. In the following stories, some of the life changes were made by our clients, some were made by us, and some were made by both. What a wonderful world!

We present you with:

Flower Shop Daughter

Women of Stature

Security Blanket Rose

The Bag of Rocks

Bridge To Peace

Moonbeam Dialogues

Flower Shop Daughter

Bonnie

I entered the flower shop with a lot on my mind. As usual, I was on a mission and feeling rushed, but as I became aware of my surroundings, I felt my pace slowing down. I inhaled the fragrance of the flowers that surrounded me. The displays looked beautiful, especially since this was November, and not much was blooming outside.

I had come to find a bouquet to send to my dear, life-long friend Sara, who had quite suddenly lost her husband. He was 68, and they had been married for over 40 years. They were in the midst of the births of three grandchildren. I was feeling so sad for her and worried about how she was doing, especially since she lived out of town and I couldn't just go and hug her.

In addition, I kept hearing the phrase in my head "There but for you go I." My husband and I have been married for 40 years and have grown children of our own. We have no grandchildren yet, but we are looking forward to that without much thought about the possibility that we might not be around for them. No wonder I was feeling overwhelmed and not very centered.

However, the flowers in the shop were helping me breathe more deeply, nurturing me, slowing me down, and making me mindful. They were pushing away the thoughts I had lately of retiring from my work as a therapist. After all, I'd listened to people's troubles for 34 years, and that is a long time. Maybe it was time to pull away and end my career. I found this to be an awful thought.

"I'm not ready," I said to myself. "What in the world would I do with my time? I love my work. But still, is it time to let go?"It remained a question in my mind even as I began to focus on selecting an arrangement for my friend, whose husband ran out of time. I looked around the shop for just the right flowers. Since winter was approaching, the shop was full of fall colors—oranges, rusts and deep yellows—the cattails, mums and autumn leaves all reminding me of the dying process. I began to feel even more sad.

"May I help you?" said the voice that came from the pretty young clerk behind the counter. She looked the picture of patience and seemed eager to attend to my needs. Her gentle smile and direct look into my eyes made me want to tell her the whole story. As a therapist who is accustomed to listening, I'm not used to hearing the words, "May I help you."

In a single breath I said, "I'm looking for flowers for my friend who suddenly lost her husband of over 40 years, and she lives out of town so I can't hug her, and I feel so bad because I'm scared that such a thing might happen to me."

And then I added quickly, "How's that for baring my soul to a stranger?"

The young woman smiled and didn't look at me as though I was crazy, much to my relief! She began to show me various arrangements as though I had made a normal request.

"Maybe your friend would like this," she said shyly. She brought out an arrangement of flowers in an antique vase. Greens surrounded the base, and candles were placed on either side of it. "I don't know, since I'm not married, but it seems to me that this arrangement might help your friend to remember that she and her husband's love will last forever. Maybe this is corny, but whenever she lights these two candles, she could think of how they lit up each others lives." She shrugged her shoulders and looked down at the flowers, blushing as she waited for my response.

I was touched by her sensitivity to my needs and her wisdom about relationships for one so young. "I'll take it," I said with little hesitation. "I love your idea! Where did you learn to be so creative about love?"

She continued to blush and offered, "I don't really know. My mom raised me all by herself, so I didn't see what marriage looks like while I was growing up. I guess I'm just impressed that people can stay together as long as you, your friend and your husbands have, and I wanted to help you honor that with your flower arrangement. I hope I can be in that kind of relationship someday." She giggled, obviously uncomfortable with all this sharing with a customer.

I laughed and said, "Thank you. You have really comforted me. I hope you can find that lasting kind of intimacy." I handed her my credit card to pay for the purchase.

She glanced at my card as her fingers moved rapidly over the cash register keys. Suddenly she stopped and looked at me with wide eyes, then spoke with a tone of wonder in her voice. "I just read the name on your card. Are you Bonnie Collins?"

"Yes," I said, wondering if admitting that was going to get me in trouble or embarass me.

"You were my mom's counselor when she was going through her divorce. I was just seven years old at the time, but I remember what a scary time that was for our whole family until my mom went to see you. Wow! I owe you my childhood. I remember even at seven years old, I was trying to protect my mom from my dad's violence by stepping between them. It was awful. I had nightmares, screaming temper tantrums—the whole bit. Then one day, my Mom came home from an appointment with you, and things began to change for all of us. She started speaking up for herself. She used a word that she said you taught her. It was the word "empowered." It is a common household word in our family to this day.

I cannot believe I have finally met you and have this opportunity to thank you. I'm 22 years old now, going to college, dating a great guy and feeling secure about myself even though a single mom raised me. I can't wait to tell her that I met you!"

It was my turn to say, "Wow! Thank you. I don't remember your mom specifically, but she sounds like she is a wonderful mother. How lucky you are! I'm glad she got so much out of therapy. Tell her I send her my love and respect."

By this time, we both had tears in our eyes, and if there wasn't a counter between us, we might have abandoned all boundaries and hugged each other. I said goodbye and thank you one more time and left the flower shop.

Now, I thought to myself, where was I? Oh yes, I was feeling a sense of loss and sadness for my friend who lost her husband. Those feelings were still there, but why had I been thinking about retirement and no longer doing counseling? After all, I have only been doing this for 34 years! I had at least 20 more to go, didn't I? My pace quickened and I eagerly headed for my day of listening.

Women of Stature

Trina

I had never worked directly with Bonnie prior to this group meeting. She had been my professor at the University of Buffalo; she went on to become my independent clinical supervisor; she became my colleague; and of utmost importance she became my friend. Years before we collaborated on *The Power of Story*, I remember being invited to her house for a group meeting of social workers. She had invited women of different clinical backgrounds to talk about issues of challenge and of magic, in their day-to-day work. We all took turns sharing why we had come to such a group, and I remember myself saying that I was a new social worker and wanted to see what the big kids were doing? Big was the operative word because I knew only Bonnie, and she seemed huge to me. She was a professor and an author and had a private practice, a family, and a demeanor that spoke of ease and comfort. I sat back for two semesters and watched how Bonnie captured her class. She virtually held us prisoner, captured by her passion, her skill and her larger than life desire for us to be as good as possible. There was nothing guarded in her giving. We were validated; we were stroked; and we were encouraged to go out and be our very best.

That is why, several years later, I was still somewhat awestruck to be invited to work directly with her. We were going to do group work with trauma survivors and their families. The event that brought these group members together was very well known; their story had captured the attention of the nation as it unfolded. Then, like many other stories, it lost momentum. Though forgotten by the rest of the world, the trauma stayed encased within its silent sufferers. They came together because there is an amazing healing quality in telling your story. It is in the telling that your soul is mirrored back by the listener. In a magical moment, there is validation that one other human being knows how I felt in that moment, in that microsecond of trauma. The teller realizes the person was not present, but in the telling and listening, constraints of time and distance are obliterated, replaced with an opportunity for the fusion of souls. In the numerous times my soul has bumped into the soul of another, both as a teller and as a listener, it has been as though the souls had no constraints of time. From a feelings standpoint it was as if the souls were equipped with centuries of wisdom. I have bumped into the soul of a six year old who possessed a soul like a revered elder. I have experienced the soul of a teenage client that possessed patience and wisdom that was well beyond her teenage years.

Because they were not allowed to connect with each other, the stories of this group of trauma survivors had been stifled. A story is meant to be told, and when it is held past term, it becomes a recipe for physical, emotional and spiritual suffering.

Sharon and her husband Mike were two of the eight participants. Mike had been a hostage and had both witnessed and suffered atrocities that pushed his coping strategies to their outermost limit. The remaining couples included another survivor and his wife, along with two adult children of hostages killed during the event, along with their spouses.

From the onset of our preliminary meetings to the actual group work, it was apparent that Mike adored Sharon, and Sharon adored Mike. The couple spoke openly and honestly about how their love for one another and their love for and faith in a power greater than themselves had allowed them to survive the horrible days during which Mike was held prisoner, beaten and shot. This same twofold love allowed them to progress through the following years and do some significant healing.

As a trauma therapist, I have learned to work from the formula that there are no degrees of horror. What I mean by that is that one person's horror cannot be compared or measured against another's. Those who suffer from afar often minimize their own experience by saying, "I didn't have it nearly as bad as the people who were actually there."

This was the case with Sharon. Sharon didn't come to this conclusion deliberately, and Mike did not facilitate it because of some subconscious need to be on center stage. As a matter of fact, Sharon didn't even know to what extent she had minimized her experience. However, it was clear that Sharon perceived that Mike had suffered more than she did.

In the course of the group, Sharon often provided us with information about the injuries that Mike had sustained, what it was like for him to learn how to walk all over again and how the personal stance he had taken as a hostage had earned the respect of some and the disfavor of others. Her speech and body language, as she offered this information, was easy and comfortable. When I first asked her what the four days were like for her, she looked as though I had hit her in the forehead with a rock. She silently stared at me. Her eyes were wide, and you could tell her mind had taken her to a different place, but she didn't respond. When I asked the question again, it startled her into a state of awareness.

With lowered eyes, she quietly responded, "Difficult, the days were difficult." She began to tell about the days, once again from Mike's perspective, and Bonnie and I gently guided her back to herself. Sharon began to speak, and a hush fell over the rest of the room as we learned about the woman before us.

Sharon talked about being a young wife and a new mother. She and Mike had a three-month-old baby girl. Mike had taken the position as a guard at a prison to earn extra money for his family. In the first hours after the prison had been taken over, there was confusion and uncertainty about who was involved. Sharon drove to the prison and stood outside with other. There they held vigil, waiting for some form of communication about the people inside whom they loved. No clear communications came, but Sharon rose to the occasion by comforting Mike's parents when they got there and then comforting her own parents. Sharon's dad had become particularly fond of Mike and enjoyed spending time with him. Sharon's older brother had been killed in a construction accident five years earlier, and as is true for all parents who have lost a child, the sting was as fresh as if it had happened yesterday.

Based on her description of the events, I could almost visualize Sharon supporting the weight and worry of these two sets of parents, who like everyone else were confused, overwhelmed and at times emotionally erratic as they searched for information. Sharon was torn as she stood vigil, sometimes overwhelmed in her fear and empathy for Mike and sometimes overwhelmed in anxiety for their little girl at home, who was away from her mother and who might very well lose her father. Little information was provided to the families, so rumor was intermingled with fact, and fact was often reduced to fiction. Nothing could be substantiated, and as minutes became hours and hours became days, Sharon held her post, exhausted, hungry and terrified.

After four days, the standoff came to a violent and sudden end. Hostages were killed; hostage takers were killed; and the area surrounding the prison became chaotic. Sharon stood motionless waiting for some word as to whether Mike had been killed or spared. When no word came, she left, went to a friend's apartment and began calling hospitals to see if Michael Smith had been brought in. It was a small community, so hospitals were being utilized in several surrounding towns. The third call revealed that

Michael had been taken to St. Jerome's, and Sharon immediately left to be with him. She raced to the hospital, and as I listened to her tell the story, I could almost see the white-knuckled grip that she would have had on the steering wheel. Her eyes would have been fixated, much like they were now as she related the memory. As Sharon spoke, it became apparent that she was no longer aware of any of the rest of us in the room. Her mind had taken her to the place of memory, where the time and distance dissolves.

When Sharon arrived at the hospital, she was fearful of what she might see, yet hopeful and happy that she was about to be reunited with her husband. As quickly as she could feel the relief, it was snatched away. Like a roller coaster heading in one direction on the straight away, then careening around the far turn and completely changing direction, her heart fell as she heard the hospital representative telling her that Michael was not there after all.

None of us in the group knew what gave her the composure to be able to do this, but she went to a phone and began the grueling task of calling all over again. Hospital phone lines in three counties were tied up. The dead, the dying and the injured were being brought to hospitals all over. Sharon finally called St. Jerome's again. Although she was sitting in their lobby, she called to see if they would again tell her that Michael Smith was there. Indeed, she was advised again that Michael Smith had been admitted, and this time she got specific information as to where he was. She was advised that Mike was seriously hurt and in surgery, so she went to the surgical suite to wait. After a short time, a nurse emerged and simply said, "Mrs. Smith, I'm so sorry. This was in your husband's pocket when they brought him in." Sharon never responded to the "I am sorry," and to this day she doesn't remember if she thought it meant Mike was dead or if she believed that the person was just expressing sympathy over the whole ordeal. Sharon only remembers being fixated on what the nurse handed her.

Sharon slowly unfolded a blood saturated note that Mike had written while he was held hostage. Some of the words were illegible, having been soaked in her husband's blood, but the majority of it she could make out. She began to read a letter of love addressed to her, their child and Michael's family. Mike had written that it was thoughts of Sharon, their daughter and his family that had given him the strength to make it through each moment, each hour and each day. Mike told her how he held on to her strength and how that kept him strong. Mike described in that letter the woman we had all come to see over the last several weeks. Sharon was strong, compassionate, giving, faithful, loving and selfless. A watercolor masterpiece that depicted love and admiration was created each and every time Mike and Sharon exchanged glances. At times it seemed that Sharon had the watercolor box and the brushes. With great courage, she nursed Mike and helped him learn to walk again, never shedding a tear that would frighten him—not even when she saw him for the first time in his hospital room. Even though she was terrified by what she saw, she never gave that fear away to Mike. Sharon walked us through those days, and many of us saw for the first time what it was like for the family members who stood outside the wall.

Many of the group members cried. Bonnie and I sat in silence waiting for the moment in which we could validate the story and touch the soul of the teller. Sometimes this happens with words, or a reframe or a glance. In this case, I knew it had to be physical. Throughout the story, I had a vision of Sharon holding up all the burdens. Perhaps in the gesture of a simple hug, some of those burdens could be channeled through me. Perhaps I could carry some of the burdens out of the room. The moment was natural; I got up and walked across the circle to hug Sharon. She simultaneously and naturally walked toward me.

I am not a particularly tall person. Throughout my adult life, my 5′ 2″ stature has served me well. My children laugh when I tell them I was the center on our varsity high school basketball team, but I could jump really high. Most people I hug are taller than I am. I had come to expect that. When you couple this expectation with my sense of greatness in the other person... well, imagine my surprise when this amazing woman, this emotional giant of a woman, turned out to be a mere sprite of a thing. I was consciously jarred when I hugged her and discovered she was significantly smaller than me. Sharon's story was so much larger than life, I assumed she was too.

I work a great deal with women and trauma. I have come to discover that some of the strongest, the ones that turn from survivor to thriver, are these women of stature. Bonnie stepped into the circle to join in the healing hug; she turned out to be smaller than me too. Imagine my amazement when she turned out to be a sprite as well. I had never thought of Bonnie as a small woman. I continue to look up to Sharon and to Bonnie as well. Perception is a very interesting thing.

I feel deeply honored to be surrounded by these women of stature.

Security Blanket Rose

Bonnie

The church was particularly beautiful—flowers everywhere, highly polished floors, stained glass windows aglow from the bright sun and soft chords of organ music interspersed with voices of the choir.

There were people everywhere. One wedding was ending as the one I was invited to was beginning. As a long line of guests left, they were passed by a line of guests arriving. Seats were exchanged so quickly they were still warm.

I stopped surveying the scene for a moment as I sought out a seat for myself. As the bride's therapist, I wanted to be unobtrusive but also in view of Judy, who I knew would be especially beautiful on her special day. I chose a seat near the aisle with a good view of the procession about to take place.

Judy had started therapy with me as a young woman of sixteen. She presented with a fairly severe anxiety disorder bordering on agoraphobia (a fear of open spaces and leaving home). She came from an exceptionally warm, empathic family, who offered her support and love of the best kind. Her parents willingly became involved in the therapeutic process and the bonding of Mom, Dad and child as a family was a joy to observe and to work with.

In family sessions, Judy's parents shared with her their own feelings and anxiety about the childhood trauma of a long hospitalization for what could have been a terminal illness. As they talked about their fears and how they never lost hope for health for Judy, she began to integrate her own feelings about such a trauma, and the anxiety began to lessen.

The therapeutic process moved swiftly from then on. Judy responded beautifully to breathing exercises, visualizations and desensitization exercises. She was able to express her fears from those early years as well as her awe at not having died. I felt that the sessions with this young girl and her parents were truly filled with sacred moments, and I was honored to be part of their healing process.

Today we were celebrating the wedding of a young woman who at one time no one was sure would live to experience it. My eyes misted as I sat in the church thinking about all of this. I focused for a moment on the altar roses and their beauty, which led me to smile at a memory of giving Judy a silk rose during a therapy session when she was looking for a security blanket to take on an airplane trip at the age of sixteen. She kept that rose for many years, and annually at Christmas, she wrote me little stories about how it would get lost and she'd go on a mad hunt to find it—and it would always be found just when she needed it most. She shared with me that it had been in many cars, planes and trains helping her get through trips, job interviews, exams and other life transitions.

As I was remembering all of this, I heard the sounds of the organ become louder, announcing that the ceremony was about to begin. With roses on the altar and roses on my mind, I turned to see Judy walking on her father's arm, a beautiful bride with a bouquet of (what else) roses. They walked to meet her new husband at the altar.

I smiled as she went by me and she smiled back. At that moment she shifted her bouquet into one hand and opened the other for a brief moment showing me the silk rose I had given her five years ago—the security blanket rose—the rose that once again was helping to reassure her that she could celebrate yet another transition in her life. Her hand closed quickly as soon as she knew I saw it, and our eyes met as we exchanged looks of knowing, of pride and of delight. I had the sense that the security blanket rose was now more of a good habit than an absolute necessity. It reaffirmed my belief in symbols and rituals as sources of healing.

The ceremony continued, and I found myself thinking about my gift to Judy and her new husband. At this moment I knew I had chosen correctly. I had given them two silk roses intertwined together in the hopes that their lives together would be so intertwined. The security blanket rose that had helped for so many years would now be joined by the new security of togetherness that I hoped this marriage would bring this young couple.

Three years later she came to introduce me to their first baby. Of course, I had a rosebud for him.

The Bag of Rocks

Trina

Olivia has dark curly hair that frames an absolutely emotionless face. If you look deeply enough into her intensely brown eyes, it is almost as if you look into a bottomless chasm. It is only occasionally, however, that you have an opportunity to look that deeply because most of the time those beautiful soulful eyes are lowered. Olivia is one of the clients who I sometimes refer to as a "shoe person." She walks through life as if she were assessing people's footwear, only occasionally darting upward glances at the people around her, and seemingly never at times when they might be looking back. Olivia was referred to our CHOICES group by her primary therapist. CHOICES is a group for women who have been impacted by childhood sexual abuse.

The therapist forewarned us, "She might not be a good fit. I can barely get her to talk in individual sessions, but maybe she will find a bond with the other women."

When we asked Olivia what she hoped to accomplish by participating in our group, she virtually whispered her response. We strained to hear her say, "I want to be able to be a mom to my boys." A single tear dropped onto the surface of the table. I asked if she would be able to look at me. For a brief moment, I saw the bottomless brown chasms fill with seeping ground waters of sadness—sadness that currently had no story. I remember my heart hurt. Sometimes my heart knows before my brain does that this story will be very painful to hear. The hurt was replaced with fear, as I wondered if I would be skillful enough to help her tell it.

Over the course of the next several weeks, Olivia remained silent. Through body gestures and symbols, we were able to get the rest of the group to bond with her, offering her patient words of encouragement like, "We will be here for you when you are ready to talk. "It's OK we can wait. Thank you for coming every week and listening to us." Sometimes there was a gentle frustration when they told her, "Please let us help you! Why won't you talk to us?"

A lot of work went into establishing a level of trust between us (the facilitators) and her. Each week, it seemed that she would make longer eye contact with me. Sometimes I could feel her eyes on me when I was working with another member. Group was moving along, almost at the halfway mark. I knew I was going to have to push a little harder.

I came in one week and waited for a member to ask the familiar, "Why won't you let us help?" As usual Olivia did not answer, so I offered a suggestion, "Olivia, I wonder if you believe you have to hold onto your pain and that you have gotten so used to holding onto it that you don't realize how heavy it is to carry?" She shrugged, and I pressed a little further. "Would you be willing to do something for me so I can experiment with that idea?"

After a long time, she said, "What?" I had filled a knapsack with stones and rocks; it was heavy to lift as I walked it over to Olivia. If you carry this around for a while you might become aware of the extra weight you carry all the time. Any time you're ready, we will be here to help you empty that satchel of pain."

I wasn't surprised when Olivia took the knapsack from me. I knew we had developed that much trust. I was surprised, though, when she walked out the door with it at the end of group.

Week after week Olivia walked in with her bag of rocks, and at the end of group she walked out with it. Week after week she paid closer attention and looked more directly as we worked with the member who was involved in the "breaking the secret" experience, which was designed to free them from the historical pain, self-blame and shame that is so often associated with childhood sexual abuse.

One week, when I was beginning to wonder if the final week of group would come and Olivia would just walk out the door with her bag of rocks, she quietly asked, "Can I share today?" It is difficult to separate the exhilaration I felt that day from the heart hurt I had felt the first day I met her. The group became quiet and prepared to listen to Olivia's story.

To my amazement Olivia sat on the floor in the center of the group, unzipped the bag, reached in and began emptying it. The fieldstones and garden rocks I had filled it with had been replaced with ornately painted and decorated bricks. One brick had been painted white; covering it were several sets of brown eyes dripping with blue tears. In bubble letters along one side of the brick was the word "SADNESS." In all there were ten or eleven bricks, each a Picasso-like masterpiece. Each carried a telling word, such as betrayal, loneliness, rage, and fear. As Olivia removed a brick she would place it on top of the one before it. The last brick she pulled out had no drawings, only one word on each surface. Every surface of the brick read "SHAME." Olivia carefully balanced the brick on the top of the pile. She silently rose and almost like a trained ballerina, she poised one foot and effortlessly toppled her wall of pain.

Bridge to Peace

Bonnie

Custody evaluations are part of my job. I don't like them much because I feel sad for the children, and no matter what the outcome, nobody is ever happy. I always attempt in this work to use language other than "legaleeze."

I talk about "parenting plans" rather than "custody arrangements." I encourage parents to rise above their own differences and all the hurt and anger they feel due to those differences and focus on their children.

I speak to them in the language of empowerment. With such language, I attempt to honor them as parents. After all, they usually know their children best. I don't want to take their power away from them if I can avoid it.

Referrals for this kind of work often come from judges who mandate that a couple going through the divorcing process come and see me. The judges, themselves, express frustration with the fact that these couples fight over their children, which slows down the divorcing process and is not good for anyone. We all know that lives lived in limbo are the most stressful lives of all.

Currently, my thoughts were on how best to explain this process to the couple in my waiting room.

My feelings didn't match my thought process. I was anxious and uncomfortable because I didn't really want the responsibility of deciding the fate of this divorcing family. (I had learned very quickly from working with people who are divorcing that it is definitely a family affair—not a process that only two people go through.) Every time I get one of these referrals, I swear I will never accept another one. The process is too sad, too full of conflict and too complex. However, I'm big on commitment, and I had made a commitment to the people sitting in my waiting room.

I took a deep breath and spent a full minute in silence at my desk with my eyes closed, attempting to ground myself in preparation for meeting this particular couple. Then I opened the door and entered the waiting room where they were sitting. They both stood up as I walked toward them and had an air of finesse and confidence I don't often see in couples who are adversaries at this point in their relationship.

Ken introduced himself first and then turned to his wife and put his hand on her back as he introduced her to me like an old-fashioned gentleman. Both Carol and Ken looked at me directly. They both shook my hand firmly.

They followed me into the therapy room, and I offered them a seat saying, "Sit anywhere. I don't have assigned seats." They both smiled and sat down next to each other on the couch.

Ken was a slim, handsome man, obviously someone who worked out. He was dressed in a tweed sport coat and khaki pants with loafers—rather preppy. He exuded confidence, which is not the norm for men coming to a therapist's office, especially around issues of custody evaluation.

His wife, Carol, was slim also and well dressed in a navy blue suit with a beautiful geometric silver pin on her lapel and small hoop earrings to match. Her hair was short and stylish; her nails were polished; and she too projected an air of confidence. She had a look of elegance and poise.

They seemed to match in their appearance and demeanor. There didn't seem to be any dissonance that would lead to divorce. My curiosity was piqued.

Of course, there was dissonance as was soon revealed in our work together. Both of these people had jobs that put them in the public eye and had what I call a "perfection persona." I wondered if it was only a persona or if it truly reflected who they were. I was soon to find out.

Before I could even begin to explain the custody evaluation process to them, Ken began to speak, "We are here because we have been recommended by our separate attorneys and the judge to get your opinion about how to handle custody of our only child, four-year-old Amy. The judge has explained your process to us, and we are eager to cooperate with it. In order to make the best use of our time, we have already talked about what we want for our daughter and have written it down for you to review and critique."

At this point, he handed me a one-page, typewritten custody arrangement. I was very impressed and somewhat shocked at such cooperation.

I was also curious about Carol's part in this and turned to her to ask if she had input in Ken's written proposal.

With a smile, looking directly at me, she said, "Yes I did. I think you need to know something about us. We are divorcing, but we are also friends. In fact, we might be better friends if we didn't have to live together. That's our hope anyway. We both love our child deeply and want to work at making this transition as easy as possible for her. We think we can do that, but we want a professional opinion on whether we are doing all we can do."

My mind raced. I needed to shift gears, relax, let down my defenses and stop trying to sell my idea of a parenting plan to these people. They were already sold on the process. I needed to honor them for their ability to rise above their differences and focus on their child. They were the ideal divorcing couple (if there is such a thing).

I glanced at the custody proposal. They had figured out a way for Amy to see both of them frequently, stay with the same preschool and continue to have the same babysitter. She could also spend time with grandparents and other relatives on both sides. This was the ideal definition of cooperation. It seemed to be the best possible situation for this family and I said as much to them.

We discussed further how to orchestrate their plan. When we were all satisfied with the results, I thought we were finished and stood up to signal the end of the session.

Carol, however, remained seated and burst into tears. This startled Ken as well as me. He had already stood to leave but sat down abruptly. He put his arm around his soon to be ex-wife and said, "Carol, what is the matter? I thought this is what you wanted. This is best for Amy, isn't it?"

Carol responded through her sobs, "Yes this is what I wanted, but it's still hard. I don't know how to go on from here. How do we live our lives now as friends instead of husband and wife? I'm crying about us, not Amy. I'm sorry. I just felt the finality at this moment, and the tears came so fast I couldn't control them."

"You don't have to be sorry," I quickly interceded. "This is a difficult time in all of your lives. It seems to me you need to honor this transition somehow."

Ken looked at me with a puzzled look on his face, cocking his head as if he was trying to look around the corner of my statement. Before he could speak, I said, "I think you two need to focus on yourselves and what this separation means to each of you. I want you to know that I believe you've done a wonderful job helping Amy get through this, and I'm sure you will continue to focus on her needs, but what about your own feelings about separating from each other?"

Carol was listening intently and had stopped crying. Ken remained with his arm around her. Looking at me, he said, in a voice filled with doubt, "What do you suggest to help us with this? It's not like a death, even though at times I suspect it's just as painful. What do we do? Have a wake and a funeral?"

I smiled at his reference to death. It was a metaphor I often used with divorcing couples. I said, "This separation is very similar to death only in some ways even harder. It seems even more difficult in your case because you truly like each other and want to remain friends. Would you like to come back for a few more sessions during which you can explore ways to say good-bye to your life together as a married couple and figure out how to go on together as friends as well as the loving parents of Amy?"

Without any hesitation, both of them nodded their heads simultaneously like two little wounded kids needing comforting.

I ended the session reaching out to shake hands with each of them but found myself embraced by Carol and connecting with Ken's handshake at the same time. It was another of what I have learned to call "holy moments" in my work.

I waited eagerly for the next session.

They returned looking as professional and as well put together as at the first visit. Again, Ken ushered Carol into the room and waited until she sat down before he joined her on the couch.

They looked at me with listening eyes, and I felt like I needed to choose my words carefully as I sensed the vulnerability under their eagerness. I said, "I'm so glad you came back. It shows such respect for each other. Whether you're married or divorced, you are each very loving to one another. How has this happened?"

Ken spoke first, "It's funny you should ask that. I think it's because we sort of grew up together. I don't mean literally. We didn't meet until we were in college, but we did seem to mature together. We have always supported each other as individuals. We cheered each other on in our professional development and were there for each other when either of us was in pain."

Carol added, "And of course parenting really bonded us in love and in anxiety for our child."

"Then why are you divorcing?" I asked, feeling quite puzzled.

The silence that followed that question was long and heavy. Neither of them spoke. Finally, Carol said in a shaky voice, near tears, "We have no passion for each other. I have never felt a desire to be intimate with Ken. I try but any physical contact numbs me."

Ken said, "Strangely enough, I feel the same way. We both decided that we want that passion, so we thought it best to release each other from our vows of marriage."

"I know," said Carol, "it could just be hormones or even trauma that blocks that passion, but we've both felt such passion with other people, so we decided it was time to go our own ways."

It was my turn to be silent. I felt in awe of their integrity and finally said, "You are very special people. Your daughter is lucky to have you as parents. I honor your decision. So now the question becomes: How do you make this transition from husband and wife to committed friends and best buddies? Maybe you need to create a "good-bye ritual" as a way of processing the end of a marriage and then an "always ritual" to honor the friendship that will go on forever."

Ken looked confused, but Carol got excited. She smiled and leaned forward in her seat and asked, "You mean like a memorial or a celebration?"

"Yes, something like that," I responded.

Then it began. It turned out that Carol was a real "ritual lady."She had made decoupages of family members who had died. She had created narrated videos with music for special events, especially if they involved their daughter. Such an idea excited her.

Ken smiled and said, "Oh boy, here we go. You have sparked Carol's love of preserving memories. This should be interesting."

The hour was up but they made another appointment in order to share with me what sort of ritual they might create.

I was eagerly curious when they returned. They seemed to step more lively as they entered the room and sat in their traditional places on the couch.

I asked, "What ritual have you created?"

Ken deferred to Carol with a hand gesture meaning "you're on!"

Carol said, "It was hard, and we actually fought about it because, as usual, I wanted to be much more elaborate then Ken did. But we finally compromised and came up with a meaningful farewell as well as a friendship commitment idea.

"So what is it?" I asked with increasing anticipation, expecting a lot of creativity from this couple.

Ken jumped in with, "Well, we've decided to throw away our wedding rings but, in a very special way. We are going to walk together to the center of our local Peace Bridge and each throw our rings into the river. We are hoping that will bring us the peace that the bridge is named for."

Carol was quiet and looked sad. She then said softly, "I think it's a good idea because even though it will be sad, it will also be good—sort of bittersweet. We then thought we'd walk back to our current home and give each other a gift to honor our continued friendship."

The session continued with small talk, appreciation for the process and a winding down of their need of me. They stood to go, and again Carol hugged me and Ken shook my hand as we parted.

I didn't hear from this couple for a long time. Then one day I got a call from Ken. He was asking for a reference for a friend, but he was also eager to tell me that he and Carol were still friends and raising Amy the best they could. I told him that I was happy for them and was still impressed by their commitment to each other and their little girl.

It was at least two years after that phone call that I got a thank you card from Carol. I thought, at first, that a thank you card seemed a bit late if she was thanking me for the transition therapy I had done with her and Ken. However, that wasn't the intent of the card.

Carol was expressing a thank you to me for approving and accepting the fact that both she and Ken had needed to separate to find themselves and to explore other relationships. She wanted me to know that they had both had flirtations with passionate relationships but had decided they found friendship to be the most important reason to make a committed relationship. Because of that awareness, they had gotten remarried. They were moving to a new city and starting a new life.

I wrote a quick note to both of them to wish them the best and suggested they walk to the center of the Peace Bridge once again and perform some sort of creative ritual to honor their new union.

Moonbeam Dialogues

Trina

The back of the van was open, and Melanie and I had finished putting the last of the cooking pans into it. Over the course of doing agency work together, Melanie and I had become both colleagues and good friends. We shared many of the same philosophies about advocating for people who are disenfranchised in some way. We enjoyed doing nice things for people, sometimes going a little out of our way for our clients. I had spent some time in Louisiana and became familiar with their philosophy of a lagniappe (a little something extra). We had just given a little something extra to our clients in the form of cooking, serving and cleaning up after an "all the fixings" Thanksgiving dinner. It was actually a couple of days before Thanksgiving, but we all pretended it was the actual day, and the women and children who were our clients ate to their hearts content. We worked in the Family Violence Program, and our caseloads consisted of women and children who had been victims of domestic violence. Many of the women had fled an abusive situation, often leaving financial stability behind them. Most of the people who attended tonight would end up with a Thanksgiving food basket from a local food pantry. We had delivered those enough to know that although generous and helpful, they usually contained small chickens, boxes of instant mashed potatoes and no pies. Maybe it was putting our slant of the world on things, but Melanie and I firmly believed that there just had to be warm-out-of-the-oven pies!

Many of the women attended a group that Mel and I led together, and their children were in a group at our agency run by Sonia, another close friend. Group members often became surrogate family to one another, so the thought of a shared "family" Thanksgiving, just felt right. We rented a lodge at a local park. The kids played board games and chased each other around. The moms visited with one another, poking their heads into the kitchen, offering to help and stealing a little taste of something just as at any family Thanksgiving dinner. A fire burned in the lodge's large fireplace, and the smell of burning logs mingled in a pleasing way with the smell of roasting turkeys. The children had made table centerpieces and were so excited to be contributors to the big dinner. We cooked, we mashed, we carved, we ate, we visited, we played, we sang. A couple of the kids stood on my feet, and we danced as the warm, rich sound of Louis Armstrong's "It's a Wonderful World" streamed from the CD player. I felt pretty good by the time the agency van left to take the last of the guests home.

As Mel and I put the remaining pots and pans in my van, I realized that for late November, it was unseasonably warm. The air was crisp, but it really wasn't cold. It was just pleasant. Actually, everything seemed pleasant.

Melanie and I sat on the hood of her car and talked. We had turned out the lights in the lodge and locked up. The car stood about twenty feet from the creek, and the moon shimmered off it. It looked like fireflies were jumping in and out of the water. The moon was enormous and full, much like my friend seated beside me. Mel was nine months pregnant, and this was the first opportunity I had to thank her for waiting to have the baby until after the big dinner. I certainly could not have done it without her. The moon shed enough light so that we could see each other clearly, yet we were wrapped in a protective shield of night. The night surrounded us full circle, beginning about twenty-five feet beyond and seemingly reaching all the way out to infinity. The night insulated us from noise or distraction. We didn't even hear the sounds of bullfrogs. I leaned back against the windshield and asked Mel if she had ever seen the lady in the moon. People are so busy looking for the man in the moon, they often miss the opportunity to see the lady. The lady in the moon made me think about strength. I am always awed by the strength possessed by the women with whom we work.

"I think they had a really good time," Mel said. I agreed and added, "It was a nice break for them, and it was almost as if some of the worry and hurt temporarily fell off their faces."

We talked about how Karen, one of the women attending tonight, had fled from Florida with, quite literally, no more than the clothes on the backs of herself and her four children. We talked about the progress she had made in finding more of herself. Karen had been a prisoner in her home. Her husband kept her so isolated, he even insisted that she home school their children. When he didn't like what she was teaching, he'd start a fire in the backyard and burn the forbidden books. When we first met the two youngest boys, they were so socially underdeveloped they wouldn't even speak. They could only dramatically cling to their mother, tremendously fearful and agitated when she was out of their sight. Tonight they played tag outside the lodge with the other children, while their mother visited with friends inside. We laughed together about Davey, the youngest; now that he was comfortable talking, we rarely could get him to shut up.

Then Melanie talked about Connie. Her arm, which was broken the last time her husband got angry with her, would be in a cast for another few weeks. She told us that this time she had kicked him out for good. It was difficult for her to take care of her three kids, but she cooked and did laundry as well as a woman can with a broken arm and a broken heart. Tonight we waited on her, and her heart perhaps healed a little as it noticed that she was important to her children and to the people around her.

We talked about the names Mel and her husband had picked for the baby. Sadie was the winning name if it were a girl. I thought Sadie was a beautiful name, yet I also thought it belonged to an older person. This made perfect sense, though, because despite our chronological ages, it often seemed like the work Mel and I did had turned us into old souls. Not old in a decrepit way, but in a wise way. Perhaps it was that innate wisdom that allowed us to embrace these infrequent moments of great goodness. Perhaps we knew it was time to take a few minutes to visit with a good friend, on a perfect night, after a perfect meal, under a perfect moon. Not all the moments we share would be this good, but these special moments would make the others tolerable. As we talked that night under the protection of the moon and our friendship, it never occurred to me that there was an unsafe conversation somewhere under that very same moon.

Sonia called early the next morning. I had taken the day off to prepare for family arriving from out of town. When she asked me to sit down, I knew the news would not be good and was frightened that something had happened to Mel or the baby. She assured me that Melanie was fine and that she had gone into labor. But she went on to say that early that morning, children cutting through a field on their way to school had found the body of a woman lying face up at the edge of a creek. It appeared that her skull had been caved in with a heavy rock that lay beside her. She probably died while Mel and I were talking the night before.

The woman's name was Lorraine. If we had served Thanksgiving dinner a year earlier, Lorraine would have been among the women attending. A year earlier, she had left an abusing husband. She stuck it out when he stalked her, even when he turned her family against her. She reported to the group that she was able to keep her composure when he picked up the children for visitation even though he screamed profanities at her. I remembered the day she telephoned me very upset. He had just called her and told her, "It doesn't matter how long it is, you bitch. I'll wait and I'll kill you."

I wondered if that is how he spoke to her the previous night, if those were the words he used. I wondered if she begged him not to hurt her, or if she cursed him back. I wondered how two conversations under the same protective moon could be so different. My conversation was with a friend; hers was with an enemy. In my mind's eye, I saw the lady in the moon—it was Lorraine. She was so strong, yet she always looked so sad.

Part Four

Self-Awareness

Writing Rituals

Introduction to
Writing Rituals

First let's ask ourselves, why write? For one thing, writing helps us focus and anchor our experiences as therapists. It makes us a witness rather than a victim or even a survivor of the trauma we hear. In the act of writing about a therapeutic encounter, an experience is reframed and retold in our language. By using our own language and writing from our own perspective, the encounter is changed from a vicarious experience to one of ownership and personalization. In this activity, the traumatic event shifts from an external locus of control to an internal locus. Ironically, this allows us to internalize an experience, detach from it and then externalize (put on paper) any trauma that is associated with the experience.

As you read our stories, we hope you will remember your own. We encourage you to create a ritual for writing. Make sure you provide yourself with enough uninterrupted time; then take the stories in your head to a place in your environment that encourages you to center yourself. You might want to play soothing music and even light a candle to get yourself in the mood for writing. Make sure you have a good pen and plenty of paper, or use a computer if you are comfortable with technology.

Write quickly using a free association style. You will find this type of writing cathartic as well as healing. The work we do with clients is by its very nature private. In addition, private practitioners are often alone in their practices, seeing client after client, unable to share their thoughts, feelings, joys and sorrows. Even the agency-based therapist is often bogged down by a huge caseload leaving little time to talk with colleagues. Writing becomes an avenue to release the remnants we are left holding when a client leaves a session.

When you have your stories preserved in writing, we hope you will read them to others in a story listeners' gathering. An outline for such a gathering follows.

The prompt questions below may enhance your ability to relate our stories to your experiences, cueing you into a internal place of personal identification. As you use the prompts, keep in mind that this is an exercise of identification, not comparison. A story born of comparison will be forced; a story born of identification will be your truth. We hope your journey from story listener to story writer and, ultimately, story teller, will be as beneficial, enjoyable and healing as ours has been.

Questions to Jog your Memory

Part I: On Being Real

- Describe a time when you set aside the rules and risked being real with a client.

- Did you feel exposed or vulnerable?

- Try to put your feelings about this into words.

Part II: Witnessing the Sacred

- Have you ever felt that you witnessed the sacred in your work?

- Write a story of that experience.

- Describe how simply being present and listening may have allowed you to feel like you were witnessing the sacred.

Part III: Making a Difference

- Describe an experience that reflects how you see the world differently because you are a therapist.

- Write a story describing an experience with a client in which you believe you made a difference.

Part Five

Story Listeners Gatherings

Two Retreat Formats for Using
The Power of Story
as a Process of Renewal
for Therapists Who Treat Trauma

Story Gathering
Retreat 1

This gathering is an opportunity for participants to share the joys and concerns that result from their work as therapists. Based on the art of storytelling, participants will be guided through a day of self-care and renewal.

Goals of the gathering

1. To come together and share stories.

2. To identify a therapist's increased risk of experiencing vicarious trauma.

3. To decrease that risk by exploring story writing.

4. To create an increased awareness that connecting with other therapists to tell our stories will reduce susceptibility to vicarious trauma.

5. To build a community of healers that may continue beyond the gathering.

Group Size

In order to provide comfortable intimacy, the gathering should be limited to 10–12 participants. It is optimal to have two facilitators to accommodate small-group process.

Time Frame

In an ideal world, this gathering could easily be a two-day retreat. However, experience has shown us that often people cannot accommodate an overnight, and we have therefore designed the retreat as a one-day gathering (9AM–4PM). One hour is allowed for lunch.

Setting

We prefer that this gathering take place in a retreat-like setting that offers opportunities for contemplation and connection. Break-out areas for personal exploration as well as community areas for sharing are encouraged. The environment, whether outside or inside, should offer physical comfort, a quiet environment, an escape from technology, yet opportunities to be stimulated by nature, color, music, aroma etc.

Materials:

Prior to attending this gathering, we suggest that participants read *The Power of Story* and complete the writing rituals. They bring this written material in the form of a journal.

Provide a CD player and CDs of soothing music, such as those by Steven Halpern and Danny Wright. Other relaxing music is available from Whole Person Associates.

Handouts and supplies needed for the experiential exercises are listed in the process section.

Process

Opening Ritual: This activity will encourage self-discovery and community-building.

- Create a sharing circle. In the center of the circle provide a candle, flowers, incense or other items to serve as a centerpiece. The centerpiece becomes the focus for the participants as they begin to develop a sense of community. Offer a moment of silence and encourage participants to go within.

Joining Rituals: After the moment of silence, engage participants in one or more of the joining rituals described below.

- **Collective Reading:** Select a poem or inspirational message to be read out loud by the group participants.

- **Introductions:** Ask the participants what they call themselves in their work. Some may call themselves counselors, some therapists, some clinicians, etc. Ultimately, whatever we call ourselves, we are all story listeners. Even though they may have never thought about it in depth before, ask participants to share how they arrived at their chosen identity word.

- **Joining Hands:** On a piece of poster board invite participants, one at time, to trace their hand. In the middle of their traced hands, have participants write their names, their most common symptom of job stress or vicarious trauma and their primary coping strategy. Make sure that each traced hand touches another hand somewhere on the poster board. Engage the group in a discussion of what people have offered.

- **Energizers and Drainers:** Using a blooming flower and a wilting flower as visual cues, have each participant hold the flowers and describe what drains them and what energizes them in their work.

Definitions: Define and describe the symptoms of vicarious trauma, and the ways in which it differs from burnout.

- Burnout can happen to any one. It's the result of heavy caseloads, mountains of paperwork, bureaucratic restructuring, poor working environments, funding cuts and other systems issues.

- Therapy can be intense and emotionally draining. Many therapists occasionally feel vulnerable, deeply sad and extremely fatigued. These, however, are not signs of vicarious or secondary trauma. It is important to distinguish burnout and transference from vicarious trauma. Burnout occurs in any occupation when there is too much work and too little support. Transference occurs when a therapist's own emotional issues are triggered by the relationship with a client.

- Vicarious trauma affects therapists who work with clients who have experienced severe trauma. It occurs when the boundaries between the therapist and the client disappear and the therapist begins to identify with the traumatic feelings of the client.

- Symptoms of vicarious trauma can include irrational fears about your own safety, nightmares that your client's story is happening to you, images of physical abuse triggered by simple affection from your loved ones and an exaggerated sense of a world gone bad. You may begin to feel that nothing in your life is as important as your relationship with your trauma clients. Your priorities change; you work much and too late; you have trauma literature on your nightstand; you can't seem to have any fun; you lose any identity other than being a trauma therapist.

Exercises: The exercises on the following pages will help participants reduce their vulnerability to vicarious trauma.

On Being Real

As suggested in Part One of this book, "being real" as a therapist does increase the risk of vicarious trauma for the therapist, but ironically, being real is also the avenue for healing from such exposure.

Process

- Ask participants to write in their journals ten words or phrases that describe themselves as therapists who are being real. (Examples: I sit on the floor; I hug my clients; I have given a client a gift; I have dropped a client a note; I have shared a personal experience with a client). Have participants pick one of these words or phrases and write a story.

  Note: It is important that you set the stage, explaining that this is free writing, gut level and intuitive. Encourage participants to not get caught up in grammar, etc. The writing is from the heart, not necessarily from the brain. Allow approximately 15 minutes for the writing of this little story.

- Each participant shares as much or as little of that story as they want. They may either read or tell their story to the group. Allow time for group reaction and sharing. This process often triggers more stories. As a facilitator, it is up to you to monitor time for this kind of sharing.

Witnessing the Sacred

The very nature of being a story listener is tantamount to being a witness. Many of the stories in Part Two of this book are about things that have merely happened in our presence rather than treatment planned by us.

Process

- Ask participants to open their journals and draw a floor plan of their office.

- Have them identify one item on the floor plan that they intentionally put into their space to create sacredness, for example, a fairy statue that suggests the possibility of magic, a book of poetry that says there is rhyme and rhythm in the universe, a vase of flowers, a piece of art.

- After identifying this item have them write a story that begins in this manner: I am the piece of art (or whatever the item might be) that you chose to adorn your sacred space. While I have resided here, I have witnessed so much that is sacred. I remember a time...

Note: Allow fifteen minutes for the writing portion of this exercise. Also, allow time for group sharing of the floor plans and stories, keeping in mind that stories often trigger other stories. You may want to mention that as participants listen to these stories, they may realize that their offices need changes to enhance sacredness. Wisely created, a setting can enhance healing; poorly created, it can predispose a therapist to vicarious trauma.

Making a Difference

We hope, as therapists, that we are making a difference by doing the work that we do. At times, however, we get discouraged and find it hard to believe that we are truly the agents of change that we want to be. The stories in Part Three of this book remind us of the "Aha!" moments in our work. It is those moments that help us cope with vicarious trauma.

Process

- Provide stones or cards with a variety of words written on them, such as hope, resiliency, loss, humility, security, faith, endurance, patience, enlightenment, empowerment, wisdom and awe.

- Have the members of the group form a circle and then place the stones or cards in the center of the circle where everyone can see them. Ask them to close their eyes and focus on an experience with a client in which they felt they made a difference for the client or during which the experience generated change in themselves.

- When they open their eyes, have them pick the word that best tells their story. The story will begin, "I remember a time when I learned about (word that they picked) or when I changed my belief about (word that they picked) or when I contributed to (word that they picked).

- Allow fifteen minutes for the participants to freely write their stories.

- Allow time for sharing and group process.

Closing Ritual

This retreat has been designed to replace vicarious traumatization with vicarious empowerment. The exercises have encouraged group members to bring what was held internally into a community of sharing. It's particularly important that this is a community of therapists. The common link we have is our profession. We know that in order to cope with vicarious trauma as therapists, we must feel the connection with other therapists, thus understanding that we are not alone. In this process, we have created a community of story listeners, who are now also storytellers. In this final ritual, we encourage group members to go forth and create their own circles of story sharing.

Process

- In advance, prepare a tray of objects that could be considered symbols of learning from this gathering. You might include items such as feathers, beads, small candles, candy, buttons, flowers, thread, string, rocks and paperclips. Three items will be needed for each group member. To provide choices, collect at least four per member.

- Provide each participant with a small box, such as an Altoid mint box or a small jewelry box. The boxes must be large enough to hold any three of the objects you collected.

- While members of the group sit in a circle, invite them to think about what they are taking away from this experience. Suggest that they think about what they have learned regarding the three themes: being real, witnessing the sacred and making a difference.

- Invite members to choose three items from the tray representing the learning they will take with them.

- Ask participants to share what each item represents as they place them in their small "story listeners" box.

- Invite each member, by name, to come forward and receive
  a single rose from the facilitators. When all members have
  come forward and are standing around the candle, which
  was lit during the opening, it should be jointly extinguished
  by all participants gently blowing it out together.

Please note that the format described above is merely an outline of
the process we use with the groups we facilitate. The experiential
exercises are suggestions and can be changed to meet the needs
of your group. Shortly after the group is formed, it will take on
a culture, a presence, a spirit of its own. We encourage you, as a
facilitator, to create many experiential exercises that will elicit the
response that you desire, while accepting that no two groups will
be the same.

Story Gathering
Retreat 2

The designs for Story Gathering Retreats are as limitless as the stories themselves. We offer another retreat as a framework that has been highly successful in our work of renewing therapists who have been vicariously traumatized.

This gathering is offered as a complete process designed for participants to share stories of trauma that they need to release from their own hearts and souls, as well as reach into the trauma and embrace the gift that the experience has given them. Based on "Trauma Rug," one of the stories in this book, participants will be guided through an art therapy project for self-care and renewal. This retreat may be offered as a followup to the first or as a healing intervention for trauma therapists. It is of particular benefit for trauma therapists who work with complex grief and with people suffering with sudden man-made or natural disasters or tragedies.

Goals for the Gathering

1. To come together and and release trauma stories that participants have not shared before.

2. To explore how listening to such stories has impacted the participants' own personal and professional lives

3. To create awareness in participants that connecting with other therapists to tell trauma stories will reduce their reaction to vicarious trauma along with the isolation that many therapists feel. In addition, the retreat is designed to normalize the emotions and responses that we all have as human beings.

4. To build a community of healers that may continue beyond the gathering.

Group Size

In order to provide comfortable intimacy, the gathering should be limited to 10–12 participants. It is optimal to have two facilitators to accommodate small-group process.

Time Frame

This is designed to be a one-day gathering, with the possibility of monthly followup sessions. These monthly sessions can allow the participants to gather and keep the "story group" going. This will help to continue the process, releasing the trauma to which they will repeatedly be exposed. We have offered this workshop from 9AM–4PM. We have also offered it from 9AM–6:30PM, ending the evening by collaborating on a shared supper. Details are left to the discretion of the facilitators as each group of presenters and participants is unique.

Setting

We prefer that this gathering take place in a retreat-like setting that offers opportunities for contemplation and connection. Break-out areas for personal exploration as well as community areas for sharing are encouraged. The environment, whether outside or inside, should offer physical comfort, a quiet environment, and an escape from technology. Optimally, the therapists attending should consider this a day off. Cell phones and pagers are highly discouraged. There should be plenty of opportunities to be stimulated by nature, color, music, aroma etc.

Materials:

- Prior to attending this gathering, we suggest that participants read *The Power of Story* and complete the writing rituals.

They should bring this written material to the retreat in the form of a journal.

- Provide a CD player and CDs of soothing music, such as those by Steven Halpern and Danny Wright. Other relaxing music is available from Whole Person Associates.

- Bring letter-size sheets of fairly heavy paper and black markers for the Silent Witness exercise.

- Cut cloth in various colors and patterns into 2 inch by 3 foot strips in preparation for making a "group trauma rug." There should be enough strips so each participant can have three to nine pieces (three if they want to make a thin braid and up to nine if they want a thicker version.

- Collect or purchase enough small stones to give each participant one during the Gift in the Trauma exercise. (Packages of stones can be purchased at most Dollar Stores.)

- Select readings identified as part of the process and make copies if needed.

- Provide boxes of tissues.

Process

Opening Ritual: This activity will encourage self-discovery and community-building.

Create a sharing circle. In the center of the circle, provide a candle, flowers, incense or other items to serve as a centerpiece. The centerpiece becomes the focus for the participants as they begin to develop a sense of community. Offer a moment of silence and encourage participants to go within.

Joining Rituals: After the moment of silence, engage participants in one or more of the joining rituals described below.

- **Collective Reading:** Distribute copies of an appropriate poem or inspirational reading that a group facilitator or participants may read aloud.

- **Joining Exercise:** Ask participants to introduce themselves and then provide an example of self-care that they currently use to deal with vicarious trauma.

- **Guided Imagery:** To help participants get in touch with their own level of pain, hurt, sorrow, loss and grief, which may be tucked within, read a guided imagery script, such as "Imagery to Support a Sense of Renewal for Therapists Who Treat Trauma." The script is included at the conclusion of this section of the book. Play soft music as you read it, using an even, neutral and supportive voice.

Transition to Awareness of Personal Trauma: After members of the group have opened their eyes, but without processing the guided imagery or breaking the silence created by the imagery, read aloud the following definitions of trauma:

- Trauma is the mental result of one (psychic) blow or series of blows, rendering the person temporariny helpless and breaking past ordinary coping mechanisms." —Lenore Terr

- Trauma is a result of either experiencing or witnessing an event that is either shocking, terrifying or overwhelming.

Introduce the Concept of Vicarious Trauma: Vicarious trauma affects therapists who work with clients who have experienced severe trauma.

- It occurs when the boundaries between the therapist and the client disappear, and the therapist begins to identify with the traumatic feelings of the cleint.

- Symptoms of vicarious trauma may include irrational fears about your own safety, nightmares that your client's story is happening to you, images of physical abuse triggered by simple affection from your loved ones and an exaggerated sense of a world gone bad. You may begin to feel that nothing in your life is as important as your relationship with your trauma clients. Your priorities change: you work too much and too late; you have trauma literature on your nightstand;

you can't seem to have any fun; you lose any identity other than being a trauma therapist.

Silent Witness Exercise: Have a participant or one of the facilitators read the poem "Existing on the Edge" (page 41).

* Distribute paper and markers. Ask participants to list three or more signs of vicarious trauma on their paper. Then ask them to hold their lists in front of them for all to see as they walk around the room in silence reading each other's lists. Allow at least 15 minutes to experience this exercise.

* Break the silence by encouraging participants to proce the feelings evoked from this silent walk.

  Adapted from *Transforming the Pain: A Worokbook on Vicarious Traumatization* by Saakvitne, Pearlman, & Staff (Norton, 1996)

Create a Trauma Rug and Share Stories: Begin by reading the Trauma Rug story, on page 56 of this book, to the group.

* Pass the basket of cloth strips among the participants, asking each person to take multiples of three strips for weaving a group rug.

* Ask participants to take turns sharing a story from their trauma work while weaving their strips into a braid. As they weave, they imagine they are weaving their trauma into the braid.

* After each story is told, the group affirms the storyteller with words such as "We honor your witnessing;" "We honor the healer within you;" "And so it is;" or other words the group may choose.

* When all who want to share their stories of trauma have done so, offer a moment of silence for the whole group.

Weave the Rug: Introduce the concept of using the braids to make a Trauma Rug.

* Ask the group to create a way to do this. Some groups will

connect all the braids into a single strand and make a circular rug. Others will weave the strands in the manner of making pot holders.

- Allow group members to create the rug in their own way.

Gifts in the Trauma: When the rug is complete, scatter the stones you purchased or collected on the rug.

- While maintaining the circle, participants sit back and share their individual reactions to the process of making the rug.

- As a way to leave the trauma in the rug and to take away a gift from being a story listener, suggest that each participant select a stone from those scattered on the rug and then share with the group what gift that stone represents. They could use the following pattern: Because of this experience, I have retrieved the gift of patience (compassion, appreciation for life, humility, etc.).

Closing Ritual: Play soft background music during this time.

- Read "I Stand in a Forest Differently" on page 79 of this book.

- Ask participants to share what they will take away from this experience.

- Together, gently blow out the candle.

Note: Be prepared to discuss what to do with the Trauma Rug. You might point out that people's sacred memories are now embodied in the rug. This usually generates conversations about what to do with the rug. Some groups may ask one participant to save it and bring it to their monthly meetings; other groups may decide to burn or bury the rug, symbolizing their disengagement from the vicarious trauma it represents.

Handout for Group Participants

Vicarious Traumatization

Definition

A transformation of the helper's inner experience, resulting from empathic engagement with clients' trauma material. It is the stress that comes from helping (or wanting to help) a traumatized person. It affects our sense of safety, trust, intimacy, competence, and belief system.

Signs and Symptoms

- No time or energy for oneself
- Disconnection from loved ones
- Social withdrawal
- Increased sensitivity to violence
- Cynicism
- Generalized despair and hopelessness
- Nightmares
- Changes in identity, world view, spirituality
- Diminished sense of competence
- Alterations in sensory experiences (intrusive imagery, dissociation, depersonalization)

Adapted from Saakvitne & Pearlman (1996)
Transforming the Pain

Handout for Group Participants

Imagery to Support
a Sense of Renewal
for Therapists Who Treat Trauma

Please allow your body to seek comfort. Shift your weight so that you feel the support of the chair you are in. Feel the sturdiness of the chair as it supports your weight. Adjust your head, neck and shoulders so you are upright but comfortable.

Slowly breathe in through your nose and gently exhale through slightly parted lips. Allow each in-breath to nurture your mind, your body, and your spirit... Exhale completely... easily... and effortlessly. Develop a rhythmic breathing pattern.

On your next in-breath, allow yourself to trace the nourishing, comforting air as it makes its way through your lungs. Convert the air to energy, allowing it to take a form or a color or a shape. Follow this energy as it leaves your lungs and radiates out into your entire chest cavity... your abdomen... your back... your hips... and your pelvis. Feel the energy as it reaches your legs, arms, ankles, wrists, feet, fingers, and toes. Take power over this energy and bring it by your own direction to areas of your body that ask for special renewal and replenishment.

On your next exhale, be aware of all the toxins that this exhale releases from your body. Visualize these toxins as they go from you, out across the room, engulfed by bubbles of healing, love and warmth, and then on to being dissipated into the universe... fully harmless in their neutralized state.

Become aware of areas of your body where toxins... pockets of isolation... or areas of resistance may prevent you from realizing the full benefit of this experience. Inhale healing energy to these places, and on your next exhale, fully cleanse and detoxify your body.

Nurture yourself in the sense of well-being that you have created. Seek out areas that you have not spent time in before. Become aware of what emotion finds its home in your abdomen. (pause)

In a safe, curious and neutral way, examine that emotion. Allow yourself to be fascinated by this new emotional body awareness.

As you continue your journey, visit your heart. Become aware of what emotion lives there and allow yourself to explore. (pause)

You now know that you can ask your body to reveal to you all of its memory, feelings, and wisdom. As you ask your body for revelations, allow it time to answer. (longer pause)

With your next deep full breath, have your energy sent to the specific place in your body where the stories of your work are held. Trusting that your mind, body and spirit will all work in harmony, follow the energy to the place that allows you to remember a specific image, story, client, word or feeling that channeled another's trauma into you. Realize that it will all be revealed in safety and support, and it will reveal itself as needed, always to be in your best interest of healing.

See yourself at that place within you... and as you do... notice that you are carrying a small satchel. Pay attention to the fabric of the satchel. What is the texture... is it colored... is there a design? Notice how light and comfortable the satchel feels in your hand.

You are at a place where you can trust this process and yourself. You possess absolute certainty that when you open the satchel, the item you need to free yourself from trauma will be revealed...

Perhaps you have a lamp that sheds light on the trauma that has been hidden in darkness within. (pause)

Perhaps you have some soothing ointment that has only needed to be applied with loving hands on the traumatic wound. (pause)

Perhaps there is a gold or silver key that allows you to unlock the lock that has kept the trauma chained within you. (pause)

You realize that with your own new-found mind, body, spirit wisdom that you may have an item of your own. Allow yourself to be free in this exploration... knowing full well that you will have the item at a time when it is needed...

If that time is now, allow the item to be revealed to you in infinite wisdom and mastery. And if that time is not now, realize that it does not have to be this moment in time. For right now, you only need to have experienced this journey to whatever point you were able, realizing there is benefit from every portion. You know you can return here at your choosing in the simple gesture of mindful breathing and energy following.

And now, taking whatever time you need... continuing to listen to the wisdom and healing energy of your body... continuing to breathe completely, fully and easily. Whenever you are ready, come back into the room. Enter gently, coaxing your eyelids to open when they are completely comfortable. Acknowledge within yourself that you have received a gift for having done this and that you are a gift for the universe.

Bonnie Collins, EdM, LCSW-R, has been a clinical social worker for thirty-five years. She practices as a family therapist and consultant to other therapists. She is also on the faculty of the Graduate School of Social Work at the State University of New York at Buffalo. In 2000, Bonnie received the "Outstanding Faculty of the Year" commendation and was given the Erie County Mental Health Association "Professional of the Year" award in 2001. She has published in professional journals and coauthored *Healing for Adult Survivors of Childhood Sexual Abuse* (Whole Persons Associates, 1998).

Trina M. Laughlin, LCSW-R, is a clinical social worker from Rochester, New York. She has over twenty years experience working with women who've been in relationships in which there was domestic violence. Her work in this field has led her to specialize as a therapist for the Society for the Protection and Care of Children, working with children who have witnessed domestic violence. In her private practice, she specializes in working with adult women who have been impacted by childhood sexual abuse. In these capacities, she was a 1998 recipient of the State of New York, Dena P. Gold Memorial Award for Outstanding Work with Women and Children. In addition, she is an adjunct faculty member in the Graduate School of Social Work in the State University of New York at Buffalo.

Printed in the United States
27837LVS00006B/304-453